Core Data

Apple's API for Persisting Data on Mac OS X

What Readers Are Saying About
Core Data

I was putting off learning Core Data—and then I saw Marcus's book. Bought it, read it, learned Core Data. It even covers the hard things I really needed to know but weren't well written elsewhere: things like Spotlight integration, version migration, syncing, and, most important for me, multithreading.

► **Brent Simmons**
Developer, NetNewsWire

If your application deals with data, you need Core Data. If you need Core Data, you need to know Marcus Zarra.

► **Mike Lee**
Engineer, United Lemur

At last we have a book to introduce people to this fantastic developer technology. Starting with a high-level overview and ending with advanced techniques, Marcus expertly guides developers on their journey from Core Data noob to expert.

► **Steve Scott (Scotty)**
The Mac Developer Network

This book does a wonderful job of leading you through Core Data's steep learning curve. Even experienced Core Data developers will learn something new.

► **Jon Trainer**
President, Outer Level

I have been using Core Data since it was introduced, and there were still new techniques that I uncovered in this book.

► **Luis de la Rosa**
Founder, Happy Apps LLC

Core Data
Apple's API for Persisting Data on Mac OS X

Marcus S. Zarra

The Pragmatic Bookshelf
Raleigh, North Carolina   Dallas, Texas

Our Pragmatic courses, workshops, and other products can help you and your team create better software and have more fun. For more information, as well as the latest Pragmatic titles, please visit us at

http://www.pragprog.com

ISBN-10: 1-934356-32-8

ISBN-13: 978-1-934356-32-6

Printed on acid-free paper.

P1.0 printing, September 2009

Version: 2009-9-22

Contents

Chapter 1

Introduction

It is hard to believe that I have been working on this book for nine months and that it is now complete. I freely admit that I walked into this project with a lot of trepidation. There was simply no way that I was going to fill an entire book about Core Data! Now looking back on it, I realize how wrong I was. If you look at Core Data in a vacuum, then it can be a fairly small subject, and believe me, that is a good thing. But when we take it as part of the whole ecology of OS X, then it becomes so much more, which makes it possible to write several books on the subject.

Back when Core Data was first introduced, I was in the process of designing a desktop application later to become known as Simple Elegant Sales. This point-of-sale software was originally written for my wife and her business as a photographer. I wanted her to be able to easily handle the accounting of her business from her laptop as she traveled from location to location. When I originally wrote the software, I had far more experience with Java than with Objective-C, but I knew that if the app was going to be taken seriously as an OS X application, the user interface had to be written in Objective-C and Cocoa. A Java UI simply would not do. However, I decided to write the back side of the application in Java so that I could take advantage of the powerful databases and relational mapping abilities of Hibernate.

I was about halfway through this project when I met Tom Harrington of Atomic Bird (http://www.atomicbird.com). He suggested that I take a look at Core Data for the back end of my software and that it might suit my needs better than Java. At that time, Tiger had not yet been released, and Core Data was still available only to developers. After experimenting with it for just one day, I immediately went back to the

> ### Joe Asks...
>
> #### Is This Book for You?
>
> If you plan on writing an application that saves data to disk, then you should be taking a very long look at Core Data. Whether you are focusing on the desktop or the iPhone, Core Data is the most efficient solution to data persistence.
>
> A good way to confirm that you know enough Cocoa to benefit from this book is to take a look at Chapter 2, *Getting Started with Core Data*, on page 7. You should find that chapter dense, but every step should be familiar to you.

drawing board, scratched the entire project, and started over. It was that much of an improvement over what I was doing.

Since that day, I have been enraptured by Core Data, and I quickly learned everything about it that I possibly could.

1.1 What Is Core Data?

In the simplest terms, Core Data is an object graph that can be persisted to disk. But just like describing a man as a "bag of mostly water," that description hardly does Core Data justice. If you've worked with Interface Builder, you know that it effectively removes a third of the coding design known as MVC. With Interface Builder, a developer does not need to spend countless hours writing and rewriting their user interface to make sure that it is pixel perfect. Instead, they simply drag and drop the elements in the IDE, bind them together, and call it done.

Of course, the problem with Interface Builder is that we still need to code the other two parts! Both the controller and the model need to be developed in code and made to work with the interface we just designed. That is where Core Data comes in. In a nutshell, Core Data removes another third from that MVC design. Core Data is the model.

It is a common misconception that Core Data is a database API for Cocoa that allows a Cocoa application to store its data in a database. Although that is factually accurate, Core Data does a lot more for us. It serves as the entire model layer for us. It is not just the persistence on disk, but it is also all the objects in memory that we normally consider to be data objects. If you have experience working with Java, C#, or some other object-oriented language, the data objects take a lot of time to write, and they are generally very repetitive in nature. Core Data eliminates most, if not all, of that boilerplate code for us and lets us focus on the business logic, or the controller layer, of our application. It does this with an interface that is as easy to use as Interface Builder.

In addition to ease of use, Core Data is also highly flexible. If we need to step in and change the functionality of some portion of the data model, we can. From how a value is handled when it is being accessed to how data is migrated from one persistent store to another, we can choose how little or how much we want to code ourselves and how much we want Core Data to do for us.

The original design and idea of Core Data came from Enterprise Objects, which is part of Web Objects, another Apple framework. You may be surprised to learn that Enterprise Objects and Web Objects, the ancestors of Core Data, still run a large portion of Apple's public-facing websites. Both iTunes and http://www.apple.com run on a Web Objects server. Therefore, although Core Data is a relatively new technology for the OS X desktop, it has a long lineage.

We are also not at the end of the story with Core Data. Although it is a stable and mature framework that is being used by thousands of applications on a daily basis, there are most certainly things coming in the future that will make it even greater. Just comparing its abilities to those of Enterprise Objects, we know that the best is yet to come. If you are starting an application now, you should be using Core Data.

1.2 In This Book

Within this book we'll build a single application that utilizes Core Data. We'll use that application as the foundation through our journey with Core Data. Once we have the application started, we'll cover a few of the technologies that are not strictly speaking part of Core Data, but they nonetheless make Core Data work. We will then start exploring Core Data in depth and how it applies to and works with the other technologies of OS X.

We will start off in Chapter 2, *Getting Started with Core Data*, on page 7, with building our demo application. In that chapter, we will go through all the steps to make our application functional, but we'll step through them very quickly. The goal of the chapter is to give us a frame upon which to build as we explore the depths of Core Data. By the end of the chapter, we will have a basic Core Data application running that we can then expand upon.

In Chapter 3, *Core Data and Bindings*, on page 27, we will explore Key Value Observing (KVO) and Key Value Coding (KVC), which are at the heart of what makes Core Data such a powerful framework. Without an understanding of KVO and KVC, the rest of Core Data will seem like magic. Therefore, we will make sure we have a solid understanding of how these technologies work and how they apply to Core Data.

Next in Chapter 4, *Under the Hood of Core Data*, on page 45, we will explore the big pieces of Core Data. We will take each component and grasp how it works with our application that we wrote and what it does in the overall Core Data framework. I strongly recommend bookmarking this chapter, because we will be utilizing its components through the rest of the book.

In Chapter 5, *Versioning and Migration*, on page 67, we will explore how to change our underlying data model once our application has been released to the public. Mistakes happen, and more often than not, improvements to an application cause a need for the data to change. In this chapter we will explore how to handle the changes to data and how to migrate it from one version to another. At the end of this chapter, we will discuss a technique that makes versioning and migration easier and reduces the amount of maintenance we need to perform.

In Chapter 6, *Performance Tuning*, on page 91, we take the components we learned from Chapter 4 and explore how to make them run as fast as possible. Although Core Data does a lot of work for us and is very performant, it is still possible to do the wrong thing and slow it down. In this chapter we will discuss some of the common mistakes made and how to avoid them. With that knowledge, we will be better armed going forward to avoid those mistakes so that we don't have to go back and fix them later.

In Chapter 7, *Spotlight, Quick Look, and Core Data*, on page 109, you'll learn about integrating our Core Data application with the rest of the operating system. Nothing screams polish to me like an application that works well with both Spotlight and Quick Look. In this chapter we will learn how to make that happen in our application.

In Chapter 8, *Sync Services and Core Data*, on page 135, we'll discuss ways in which we can sync the data that is in our application across multiple instances. With more and more users having more than one computer, it is ever more important to be able to keep data "in the cloud" and sync it properly across machines. By the end of this chapter, we will be able to add that functionality to our application.

In Chapter 9, *Multithreading and Core Data*, on page 157, you'll see how to maximize the use of the computing power available to us. Modern desktops and laptops have more than one CPU available to use, and if the situation demands it, it is expected that our applications will take advantage of all that processing power in a parallel manner. In this chapter, we explore the safe ways to make a Core Data application multithreaded.

In Chapter 10, *Core Data and iPhone*, on page 179, we take a side step to discuss how we can use the power and flexibility of Core Data to make our iPhone development easier. In this chapter we will also be introduced to a new controller object that does not currently exist on the Desktop.

In Chapter 11, *Recipe: Distributed Core Data*, on page 203, we explore one solution for using Core Data across a distributed environment. By combining Core Data, Bonjour, and distributed objects, we can access a Core Data repository from more than one client spread across a local network. Although I would not recommend developing the next great MMORPG with this solution, it certainly has its uses.

In Chapter 12, *Recipe: Dynamic Parameters*, on page 225, the final chapter, I share one of my secrets that I used in Simply Elegant Sales and have used several times since its original design. In this recipe, we design a document-level properties storage system similar to NSUserDefaults.

By the end of this book, we will have a superior grasp of all that Core Data can do along with many practical applications of this technology. From here we can take that knowledge to build the next generation of fantastic desktop applications.

1.3 Acknowledgments

When I first started working with Core Data, I enjoyed it so much that I wanted to share all the discoveries that I had made with it. I soon continued sharing discoveries with other technologies as my enjoyment of the sharing became addictive. A while back I had the pleasure of meeting a fellow developer by the name of Matt Long and helped him become more proficient with Cocoa and its related technologies. During that time, we continued to share what we were learning and teaching in the form of the blog "Cocoa Is My Girlfriend." All of that led to this book. What started out with a simple altruistic gesture has turned into the text you are about to enjoy. Along the way I have been helped by a number of fantastic developers.

First, I would like to thank Matt Long for convincing me to share what we learned in a broader space than just one on one. I think that discussion has changed both of our lives forever.

Second, I would like to thank Tom Harrington for turning me on to Core Data in the first place. Being pointed at this technology at that particular time had a drastic positive change on my development efforts at the time.

I would also like to thank one man who tends to remain behind the scenes: Brent Simmons. A quote comes to mind when I think of Brent: "Keep away from people who try to belittle your ambitions. Small people always do that, but the really great make you feel that you, too, can become great." —Mark Twain. Thank you, Brent, for making me feel that I, too, can become great.

Lastly, I would like to thank the reviewers of this book who have caught, corrected, and pointed out my many mistakes while writing. As every developer knows, it is nearly impossible to test your own code, and the same goes for your own writing. Without the people who read this book and tested the code while it was being written, this would be a far inferior work than the one you have in front of you. The testers and reviewers of this book have gone further than I ever expected to help make sure this work is accurate.

Chapter 2

Getting Started with Core Data

Instead of starting off discussing theory or reviewing the concepts be-hind Core Data, we will dive right into writing a Core Data application. The application we build in this chapter will be used throughout the rest of the book to explore the intricacies of Core Data.

You will be learning through doing. We will build a basic application and, in the chapters following, look back through it to understand what the pieces actually do. In this book we are writing a food recipe appli-cation that uses Core Data. The concepts within a recipe application are well known, and we will avoid spending cycles on trying to figure out the concepts of the application while also trying to grok Core Data itself.

2.1 Our Application

Before we start building our application, we will do a quick overview of how the UI will look and work (see Figure 2.1, on the following page).

In section 1, we will allow the user to edit information about individual recipes. Each recipe can be selected in the list and its details edited next to it.

In section 2, we will allow the user to enter the ingredients of the selected recipe. Each recipe will have its own list of ingredients that can be added, viewed, and edited here.

In section 3, we will allow the user to add a picture of the recipe for reference. This is a view-only element, and the addition of the image will be handled through the main menu.

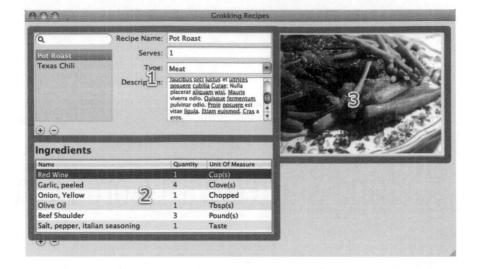

Figure 2.1: OUR RECIPE APPLICATION

2.2 Our Application Design

In this chapter, we will start at the very beginning. You will be launching Xcode and proceeding through all the steps to create the application and bring it to a usable state. At the end of this chapter, you may be surprised that the steps to create our application are so few. This is part of the allure and strength of Cocoa development. Coupled with Core Data, it is doubly so.

In the first version of our recipe application, we will give our future users the following abilities:

- The ability to add recipes with a description, type, name, image, and number of people it serves

- The ability to add ingredients to those recipes that include a name, quantity, type, and unit of measure

This first version of our application is intentionally simple. This is useful both so that we can add features to it later and thereby explore some of the abilities of Core Data and so that we can keep the distractions to a minimum while we explore Core Data.

2.3 Advanced Readers

If you are already a bit familiar with Core Data and building a Core Data application, please feel free to move quickly through the rest of this chapter. In this chapter, we will walk through the construction of our project and how to build its data model. The end result will be a data model like the one shown in Figure 2.4, on page 14.

2.4 Creating Our Xcode Project

The first step is to create our Xcode project. With the recent versions of Xcode, quite a few project templates are available to us, and more than one of those is based on Core Data. If you are using Leopard, then you will want to use the Core Data Application template, and if you are using Snow Leopard, then you want to select the Cocoa Application template and ensure that the "Use Core Data for storage" checkbox is selected.

Once we select which template, we will name the project Grokking Recipes, which will also be the name of our application.[1] In your Groups & Files listing in Xcode, you will see an additional folder named Models containing the data model file (see Figure 2.2, on the following page).

The basic Core Data template gives us an application that works somewhat like Address Book. In Address Book, the user has only one data file and generally accesses that data file via one window. Our recipes application will be designed around that same pattern. We will have exactly one data file that all the user's recipes will be stored in.

Once the project is created in Xcode, it is time to start building the Core Data aspects of our application.

2.5 Building the Data Model

Core Data applications are like database-driven applications, and in that light, we will start with building the data structures first and then move to the user interface. The three components we are going to be working with at this point are entities, attributes, and relationships.

In our design (see Section 2.2, *Our Application Design*, on the preceding page), we already described at least two of the data objects that we

---

1. Although it can be changed later.

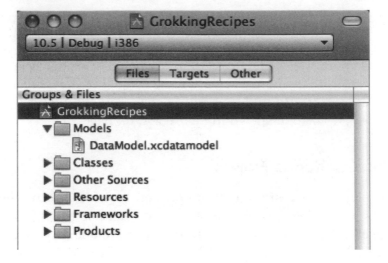

Figure 2.2: THE DATA MODEL IN XCODE

want to use and at least some of the attributes. Therefore, we will start with them. In our Xcode project, there is a group called Models, and within that group is a file called DataModel.xcdatamodel.[2] This file is a representation of the data structure that Core Data will use. This file has a lot of similarities to an entity-relationship diagram (ERD) except that Xcode will compile it directly into our final data file structure.

Adding an Entity to the Model

In Core Data, an entity has a lot of similarities to a table in a normal database design. Although this similarity is not exact, it is a good place to start.

To add our first entity to our data model, first open the .xcdatamodel file in the Models group, and then choose Design > Data Model > Add Entity from the menu bar (or use the + button in the entry area in the top left). This will add a blank entity to our data model. Next, double-click the name of the entity, and rename it to Recipe.

---

2. It is possible this file will be named ${PROJECT_NAME}_DataModel.xcdatamodel depending on the version of Xcode you are using.

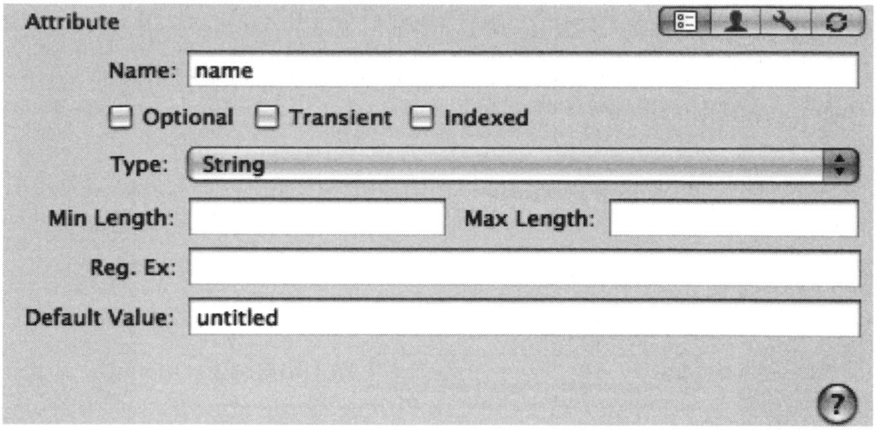

Figure 2.3: ATTRIBUTE DETAILS

Adding an Attribute Property

Just as an entity has a lot of similarities to a table, a property has quite a few similarities to a column in that table. This similarity breaks down very quickly when we start adding relationships, but it helps in the beginning to think of it this way. Properties are further broken down into several subtypes; the two most relevant are attributes and relationships. Relationship properties describe the relationships between two entities, and attribute properties are the values of an entity.

To add our first attribute property to our Recipe entity, select the entity, and choose Design > Data Model > Add Attribute from the menu bar; you can also use the top + button or the keyboard shortcut. Like the entity creation, this will create a new attribute property within our entity. Double-click the name of this property, and rename it to name. After renaming the attribute, select it to see its details, as shown in Figure 2.3.

These details allow us to control several aspects of the attribute including the default value, what type of attribute it is, and whether it is transient, indexed, optional, and so on. We will go through all of these settings in greater detail later, so for now set the type to String, set the default value to untitled, and make sure it is not optional.

Once the first attribute is finished, add the following attributes to the Recipe object:

- Set imagePath to an optional String without a default value.
- Set desc to an optional String without a default value.
- Set serves to an Integer 16 with a minimum value of 1 and a default value of 1. Be sure to flag it as nonoptional.
- Set type to an optional String with a default value of Meat.

Creating Our Second Entity

With the Recipe entity nearly complete, it is time to create our second entity. This second entity will store the ingredients that go into a recipe, and we will call it RecipeIngredient. Following the same steps, we can add these attributes:

- Set name to a nonoptional String with a default value of untitled.
- Set quantity to a nonoptional Integer 16 with a minimum value of 0 and a default value of 1.
- Set unitOfMeasure to a nonoptional String with a default value of untitled.

Adding a Relationship Property

Relationship properties are created in the same way as attribute properties, although the specifics naturally differ. Add a relationship to the Recipe entity by selecting Design > Data Model > Add Relationship from the menu bar. For this first relationship, name it ingredients, and flag it as optional.

Where a relationship is different from an attribute, however, is in the properties. Instead of defining an object type, default values, and so on, we are instead defining a destination entity, an inverse relationship, and whether this relationship is "to-many." For this relationship, we will start by naming it ingredients, and then we set the destination entity to RecipeIngredient, but we are not going to set the inverse relationship yet. We are also going to flag it as to-many, since a recipe can definitely have more than one ingredient.

The last option, the delete rule, instructs Core Data on how to handle the relationship when this, the Recipe entity, is deleted. In this relationship, we will delete the RecipeIngredient object to avoid any disconnected objects. Therefore, we will select the cascade option, which will remove any associated RecipeIngredient objects when the Recipe entity is deleted.

Joe Asks. . .

What Is One-to-Many?

One-to-many is a database term that describes the relationship between two tables in the database. Normally, there are three kinds of relationships: one-to-one, one-to-many, and many-to-many. A *one-to-one* relationship means that for each record in the first table there can be no more than one record in the second table. In a *one-to-many* relationship, for each record in the first table, there can be more than one record in the second table. The last relationship type, *many-to-many*, means that for any record in the first table, there can be any number of records in the second table, and, likewise, for each record in the second table, there can be any number of records in the first table.

Completing the Relationship

One rule that is often repeated by the developers of Core Data is that every relationship in your database should have an inverse. Although this may not make logical sense for the data, it is important for data integrity within Core Data. What this means from our programming perspective is that we need to be able to reference each object in the relationship from either side. Apple recommends this inverse relationship for many reasons, which will be discussed in greater detail throughout this book.

To set up the inverse relationship, we select the RecipeIngredient entity and add a Relationship property to it just like we did in the Recipe entity earlier. This new Relationship property is named recipe with a destination of the Recipe entity. Next, we set the inverse relationship to be ingredients, which was the name of the relationship we set in the Recipe entity. As soon as we set the inverse relationship on the RecipeIngredient, the graphical view of the relationships will change. Instead of two lines connecting the objects, they are replaced with one line, making the graphical view quite useful for debugging relationship settings. In our current design, an ingredient can have only one recipe; therefore, we leave the to-many option unselected. Lastly, we set the Delete Rule setting to Nullify. This setting will not delete the Recipe entity when a RecipeIngredient object is deleted. Instead, it will just break the connection between the two.

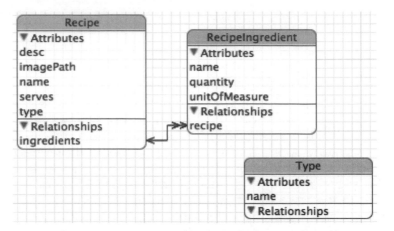

Figure 2.4: THE MANAGED OBJECT MODEL (MOM)

Adding the Last Entity

We have one more entity to add in this release of our recipe application. We will be categorizing the recipes that are added. For example, we will be separating desserts from appetizers, and so on. To keep these categories consistent, we store the actual category names in their own object. Therefore, add one more entity to our model called Type. This entity has only one attribute property, called name, which is a nonoptional string with no default value. Lastly, this entity has no relationships because it will be used only as a lookup to populate the type NSComboBox discussed in Section 2.7, *Adding the Recipe Details*, on page 20.

And with that last entity, that concludes the construction of the data model for our application. The final result should look similar to Figure 2.4.

Build the Data Objects

In other languages, or even in Cocoa applications that do not use Core Data, the next step would normally be to build the data objects that are associated with the "tables" in the "database." Fortunately, we are working with Core Data, and there are no data objects to construct. As part of Core Data, defining the data model also defines the base data objects for us. If we need custom management of objects, we can extend from these, but at this point the base data objects (called NSManagedObject) are more than sufficient for our needs.

2.6 Building the Controller Layer

As you know from your experience developing Cocoa apps, Interface Builder is a very large part of any project. Now that we have built our data model and we have a template ready in Xcode, it is time to put together the user interface.

I should mention two things before we get into the fun of Interface Builder:

- This is not going to be Delicious Library. We will be using standard widgets for our application to help keep the non–Core Data code to a minimum.

- There are a *lot* of features that we *could* add to this application but we won't. Those features, although useful, will detract from our focus.

Adding Objects to the xib

The first part of the user interface we will work on is the objects in the xib file. As with most applications, we need to add the AppDelegate to the xib so that it both will be instantiated on startup and will be properly linked into the application itself.

Add the AppDelegate

Upon opening MainMenu.xib and depending on the whims of the templates within Xcode, the AppDelegate may already be in the xib file. If it is, great! Move on to the next section. If it is not, then we need to add it.[3]

To add the AppDelegate to the xib file, follow these steps:

1. Find the NSObject in the library palette, and drag it to the xib's window.

2. Click the name of the NSObject, and when it is editable, change it to AppDelegate.

3. Go to the Identity tab on the Inspector palette, and change the class of the object from NSObject to AppDelegate.

4. Right-drag from the application to the AppDelegate object, and select Delegate.

---

3. Please note that depending on the version of Xcode you are running, the application delegate could have the application name prepended to it. If it does, then please substitute that name for any reference to AppDelegate in this context.

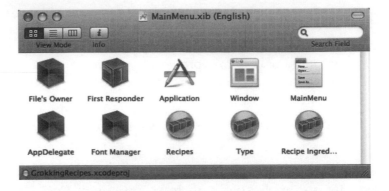

Figure 2.5: The main menu xib

When this is completed, the AppDelegate class will be instantiated when our application launches, and the application will send all delegate messages to it.

Adding the NSArrayController Objects

Our application is going to display all of our recipes in a single window. To do that, we need to be able to reference the data so that it can be displayed. Therefore, add three NSArrayController objects into our xib that reference that data. Our window will then reference those NS-ArrayController objects. Once the NSArrayController objects are added and configured, the xib will look like Figure 2.5.

To add an NSArrayController for the recipe entities, follow these steps:

1. Find the NSArrayController object in the library, and drag it to the xib file.

2. Click the name of the NSArrayController, and when it is editable, rename it to Recipes. If you have trouble getting the element to go into edit mode, you can change the name in the Identity inspector in Interface Builder and change the identity Name field.

3. On the Attributes tab of the inspector, change the mode from Class to Entity, and change the entity name to Recipe.

4. Make sure that the Prepares Content flag is selected.

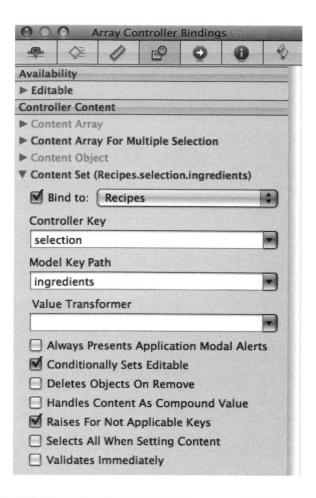

Figure 2.6: NSArrayController CONTENT SET PROPERTIES

5. On the Bindings tab of the inspector, bind ManagedObjectContext to the AppDelegate with a model key path of managedObjectContext.

Now that we have the recipe's NSArrayController built, we need to configure the other two, the recipe ingredients and the type. The type NSArrayController follows the same steps as our Recipe entity, but we need to set the entity name to Type so that it will be populated with Type objects. Other than that one difference, we can follow the previous steps to complete the type's NSArrayController.

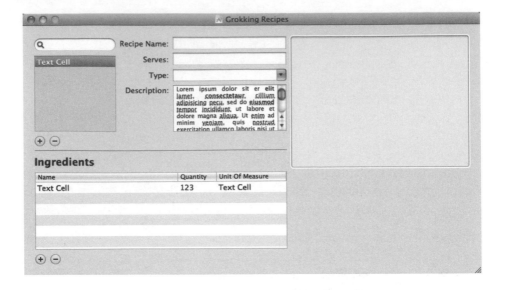

Figure 2.7: THE MAIN WINDOW

Set the identity of the last NSArrayController, the recipe ingredients' NS-ArrayController, to RecipeIngredient. In the Attributes inspector, choose Entity, and set the entity name to RecipeIngredient. Set the bindings as before with one additional change. On the Bindings tab of the inspector, enable the content set in the controller content and point it at the recipe's NSArrayController with a controller key of selection and a model key path of ingredients. See Figure 2.6, on the preceding page.

Now we are ready to build the NSWindow itself.

2.7 Building the User Interface

Now that we have all the data objects referenced properly, it is time to build the user interface. Although this interface certainly will not be winning any ADAs[4] any time soon, it will allow us to view and edit all the data objects in our model. The window we are building will look like Figure 2.7, and we will quickly walk through the steps to set it up with a more detailed review of what we are doing in Chapter 3, *Core Data and Bindings*, on page 27.

---

4. Apple Design Awards

Building the Recipe Source List

The first part of this interface that we are building is in the upper-left corner just below the search field. This view is an NSTableView that is configured with one column, no horizontal scroll bar, an automatically displaying vertical scroll bar, and the highlight set to Source List. The scroll bars are configured in the inspector for the NSScrollView. The number of columns and the highlight option are configured in the NSTableView inspector. Each of these inspectors can be accessed by Control+Shift-clicking (or Shift+right-clicking) the NSTableView and selecting the appropriate view from the list. If the inspector is not on the screen, it can be displayed from the Tools > Inspector menu item.

To bind this table to our recipe's NSArrayController object, though, we need to dig down a little bit and get ahold of the NSTableColumn so that we can tell that column what to display. We could click in the table view until eventually, ideally, we would get the NSTableColumn selected, but fortunately there is an easier way. If we Shift+right-click the table, we will be presented with a pop-up listing all of the views, hereby making it easy for us to select the NSTableColumn (see Figure 2.8, on the next page). With the NSTableColumn selected, we can now open its Bindings tab in the inspector and bind its value to the RecipesNSArrayController with a controller key of arrangedObjects and a model key path of name. Once this is set, our Recipe entities will now show up in this table. More important, when we click a recipe in this list, that recipe will become the selection that feeds the rest of the UI.

Next we need to add the buttons that will control the creation and removal of Recipe entities. To do this, we drag an NSButton (it does not matter which one) from the Library and place it below the Recipe table view. Then in the button's Attributes tab, we want to set its image to NSAddTemplate (a system-level image available for our use), change its style to Round Rect, and remove its title if it has one. Once that is done, we need to select the menu item Layout > Size to Fit to get the button to the perfect size. Once that is done for the add button, select Edit > Duplicate from the main menu to create a second button and change the second button's image to NSRemoveTemplate.

Next, we can "wire up" the buttons under the NSTableView and connect them directly to the recipe's NSArrayController. The add button will be connected to the -add: action, and the remove button will be connected to the -remove: action on the Recipes NSArrayController. These buttons can be connected to their actions by holding down the Control key,

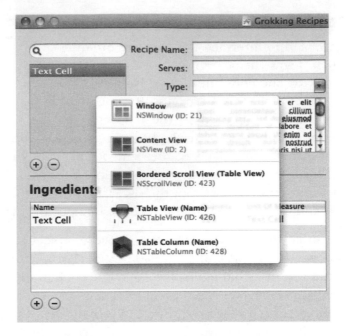

Figure 2.8: LIST VIEW TREE

clicking the button, and dragging from the selector sent action to the NSArrayController. With those small changes, we can now add and remove recipe entities at will.

Adding the Recipe Details

With the source list in place, it is time to add the details about the recipe. These details, specifically the name, serves, description, and type, will tie to the now-valid selection controller key on the recipe's NSArray-Controller. That way, when a user clicks in the list, the relevant details of that recipe will be selected.

The first two are text fields, and the third is a combo box, as shown in Figure 2.7, on page 18. With the exception of the combo box for the type, all of these details are configured the same way. All of them have their Value binding associated with the recipe's NSArrayController object with a controller key of selection and a model key path of name, serves, and description as appropriate. One tip with regard to the text area is to be sure to turn off the Rich Text setting. With this setting on, the field expects an NSAttributedString instead of an NSString and can be a bit

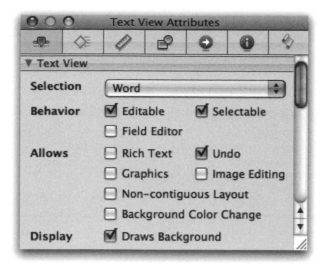

Figure 2.9: REMEMBER TO TURN OFF THE RICH TEXT SETTING.

confusing (see Figure 2.9). In addition, to be proper citizens, we should drag over an NSNumberFormatter to the Serves text field and configure it to allow only whole numbers.

The combo box is a little more complex. Although it is also associated with the selected recipe, we need to populate the entire list with values. For now, we will enter the possible values for this box manually into Interface Builder, as shown in Figure 2.10, on the following page. Next we need to bind its current value to the selected recipe. We do this by binding the NSComboBox value to the currently selected recipe's type value. On the Bindings tab for the NSComboBox, we open the Value section, bind it to the recipe NSArrayController, and set the controller key to selection and model key path to type. Later, in Section 4.4, *NSManagedObjectContext*, on page 58, we will show how to prepopulate this list directly into the Core Data persistent store.

Adding the Ingredients

Now that we have the recipe section of our UI complete, it is time to add ingredients. This is the table you see in the lower-left corner of our window. Fortunately, this part is almost identical to setting up the

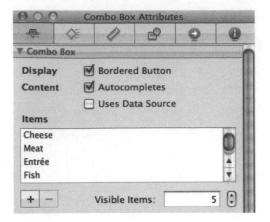

Figure 2.10: MANUAL DATA ENTRY FOR THE COMBO BOX

recipe source list. However, unlike the recipe source list, our NSTable-View will have three columns, display its headers and its vertical scroll bar, but hide the horizontal scroll bar. Enter the column headings as Name, Quantity, and Unit of Measure.

Like the recipe source list, bind the values for each column in the NS-TableView to our recipe ingredients' NSArrayController using the controller key arrangedObjects and using the appropriate model key paths: name, quantity, and unitOfMeasure. The quantity column (or more specifically the table cell in the quantity column) should also have an NSNumberFor-matter assigned to it so that the quantity is properly formatted for the value that it holds. Once those are configured, we can see the recipe ingredients for the selected recipe. Remember that we configured the recipe ingredients' NSArrayController to feed off the selected recipe, so we do not have to do anything extra at this point.

Like the recipe source list, the add and subtract buttons are config-ured by binding them to the recipe ingredients' NSArrayController objects -add: and -remove: methods, respectively. And with that, we have the ingredients section complete and are nearly done with our UI.

2.8 Adding a Splash of Code

Wondering where the code is? As it stands right now, our recipe appli-cation is fully functional. We can run it without any actual code on our part and start inputting recipes. With the combination of Cocoa and Core Data, we can produce an application like this with no custom code on our part. However, we are not stopping there.

Displaying a Picture of the Recipe

What recipe application would be complete without a picture? The users of our application need to know what the dish is going to (or at least *should*) look like when they are done. Fortunately, from the UI point of view, this is an easy addition. Drag an NSImageView (referred to as an *image well* in Interface Builder 3.1) onto our window, and connect its value path to the imagePath of the recipe's NSArrayController with a controller key of selection.

Importing Images

Once we have the NSImageView added to our user interface, we need to make our AppDelegate aware of it. In addition, we need to add a way to *set* the image path of our Recipe entities. Therefore, we need to update our AppDelegate.h and add an IBOutlet for the recipe NSArrayController and an IBAction to be able to set the image path, as shown here:

GrokkingRecipes_v1/AppDelegate.h

```
@interface AppDelegate : NSObject
{
  IBOutlet NSWindow *window;
  IBOutlet NSArrayController *recipeArrayController;

  NSPersistentStoreCoordinator *persistentStoreCoordinator;
  NSManagedObjectModel *managedObjectModel;
  NSManagedObjectContext *managedObjectContext;
}

- (NSPersistentStoreCoordinator *)persistentStoreCoordinator;
- (NSManagedObjectModel *)managedObjectModel;
- (NSManagedObjectContext *)managedObjectContext;

- (IBAction)saveAction:(id)sender;
- (IBAction)addImage:(id)sender;
@end
```

The IBAction, specifically -(IBAction)addImage:(id)sender;, will be called from our main menu and will display an open file dialog box when it is called. In addition, for us to be able to work with the recipe entities, we need to be able to get a reference to the selected recipe. To do that, we will add a reference to the recipe's NSArrayController that is instantiated in our nib within the AppDelegate.

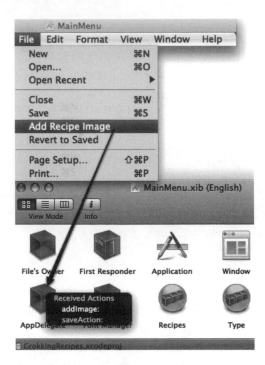

Figure 2.11: ADD RECIPE IMAGE MENU ITEM

Once the recipe's NSArrayController has been added to the AppDelegate header, we need to go back to Interface Builder briefly and Control+drag from the AppDelegate to the recipe's NSArrayController to complete the binding.

While we are here, we need to add a menu item to the File menu. We do this by making sure the MainMenu element is open in Interface Builder (it will appear as a floating menu) and clicking its File menu. From there we can either add a new NSMenuItem or use one that already exists that is not being used. Since the Save As menu item is not relevant to our application, go ahead and rename it to Add Recipe Image. Once it is renamed, Control+drag from it to the AppDelegate, and bind the menu item to the IBAction we defined in the header, as shown in Figure 2.11. With the bindings in place, it is time to implement the -addImage: method.

```
- (IBAction)addImage:(id)sender
{
  id recipe = [[recipeArrayController selectedObjects] lastObject];
  if (!recipe) return;

  NSOpenPanel *openPanel = [NSOpenPanel openPanel];

  [openPanel setCanChooseDirectories:NO];
  [openPanel setCanCreateDirectories:NO];
  [openPanel setAllowsMultipleSelection:NO];

  SEL select = @selector(addImageSheetDidEnd:returnCode:contextInfo:);
  [openPanel beginSheetForDirectory:nil
                               file:nil
                      modalForWindow:window
                       modalDelegate:self
                      didEndSelector:select
                         contextInfo:recipe];
}
```

The implementation of -addImage: will display an NSOpenPanel, which
will attach to the window as a sheet, making it modal to the window.
Next, we tweak the NSOpenPanel a little bit so that it cannot select direc-
torics or multiple files or create directories. You will also notice that we
first check to make sure a recipe has been selected before we open the
panel. A little bit of error checking can go a long way.

Since sheets work asynchronously, we need to hand it a callback to
another method in the AppDelegate. Also, while we are engaging the
sheet, we will pass along the current recipe reference. When the sheet
calls back, we are guaranteed to still be talking about the same recipe
we started with.

```
- (void)addImageSheetDidEnd:(NSOpenPanel*)openPanel
                 returnCode:(NSInteger)returnCode
                contextInfo:(NSManagedObject*)recipe
{
  if (returnCode == NSCancelButton) return;
  NSString *path = [openPanel filename];

  //Build the path we want the file to be at
  NSString *destPath = [self applicationSupportFolder];
  NSString *guid = [[NSProcessInfo processInfo] globallyUniqueString];
  destPath = [destPath stringByAppendingPathComponent:guid];
  NSError *error = nil;
```

```
  [[NSFileManager defaultManager] copyItemAtPath:path
                                          toPath:destPath
                                           error:&error];
  if (error) {
    [NSApp presentError:error];
  }
  [recipe setValue:destPath forKey:@"imagePath"];
}
```

In -addImageSheetDidEnd:returnCode:contextInfo:, we grab the filename from the NSOpenPanel and stick it into the correct recipe. As part of this callback, we get passed the recipe so we will get the filename and set it into the recipe. However, there is a risk there. What happens if the user moves the image? Perhaps it was a temporary image? To ensure that we always have the image available, we will copy it to a known location within our control and then use *that* file path. To accomplish this, we grab the filename from the NSOpenPanel and also construct a unique path within our Application Support directory structure. Next we use the NSFileManager to copy the image to that location. Last we set the new file path into our Recipe object.

With the addition of that menu item, we have completed the initial functionality. Our application is now ready to hand off to our trusty users, and we can eagerly await feedback. While we wait to hear back from them, we can tear into the depths of Core Data. To test our application, we can do a Build and Go from Xcode and start entering recipes into the application.

Chapter 3

Core Data and Bindings

Cocoa Bindings provides a lot of the magic behind Core Data. Cocoa Bindings consists of a number of APIs and concepts that together allow us to develop our applications using the Model View Controller paradigm without requiring a tight coupling of the three aspects.

Cocoa Bindings allows us to design views, controllers, and models that all expect data in a specific format without requiring that we bind them to specific classes. This means we can use views in multiple places and swap out controllers and even models without extensive (if any) recoding.

In this chapter, we'll look at some of the key components of Cocoa Bindings and then delve into the specifics of how Core Data works with those bindings. The two primary APIs that we are looking into are Key Value Coding and Key Value Observing. Between these two APIs, we are given a tremendous amount of flexibility in our design. In addition, these APIs are part of the foundation that allows Interface Builder to function and allows us to focus on the business logic of our applications. Lastly, these APIs are used heavily by Core Data to allow us to focus on the business logic of our applications as opposed to the data layer.

3.1 Key Value Coding

One of the cornerstones of Cocoa Bindings is Key Value Coding (KVC). Key Value Coding is a way to access the attributes of an object without calling the accessors of that object directly. Key Value Coding is implemented through an informal protocol on NSObject itself and is used mainly through the getter/setter pair -valueForKey: and -setValue:forKey:.

-valueForKey:

The method -valueForKey: is a generic accessor to retrieve an attribute on an object. For example, if we had an object called Recipe and it had an attribute called name, normally we would access that attribute via the following:

```
Recipe *myRecipe = ...
NSString *recipeName = [myRecipe name];
```

However, this requires specific knowledge about the Recipe object to exist in the calling method and generally requires that we import the header file of the Recipe object. However, with Key Value Coding, we can obtain this same attribute without having any preexisting knowledge about the Recipe object:

```
id myRecipe = ...
NSString *recipeName = [myRecipe valueForKey:@"name"];
```

By itself, this is not all that useful. However, there are huge benefits to it that are not apparent on the surface. Here's an example that shows how you might better take advantage of this:

```
- (NSString*)description
{
  NSMutableString *string = [NSMutableString stringWithFormat:@"[%@] {",
    [self class]];
  NSEntityDescription *desc = [self entity];
  for (NSString *name in [desc attributeKeys]) {
    [string appendFormat:@"\n\t%@ = '%@'", name, [self valueForKey:name]];
  }
  [string appendString:@"\n}"];
  return string;
}
```

In this example, I am utilizing the NSEntityDescription[1] class to retrieve the names all of the attributes of an NSManagedObject subclass and generating an NSString for display in the logs. With this method, I can reuse it in every NSManagedObject subclass that I create rather than having to create a custom -description method for each subclass.

There are a couple of things to note in this example. First, the target object is not required to have accessor methods for the attribute being queried. If our target object has only an ivar[2] for a name, it will still be resolved and retrieved properly. In addition, if the target object

---

1. We will discuss the NSEntityDescription class in greater detail in Chapter 4, *Under the Hood of Core Data*, on page 45
2. ivar stands for instance variable. This is different from a static or local variable.

has neither an accessor nor an ivar, the target object will still have a chance to respond to the request before an error occurs via the -valueForUndefinedKey: method. Lastly, all the properties of an NSManagedObject are queryable via the KVC protocol. What this means is that if we have an NSManagedObject defined in our model, we can retrieve an instance of that object and access its properties without having to implement a *single line of code* in the target object!

-setValue:forKey:

Being able to dynamically access properties on an object is quite useful, but that is only half of what KVC does. The other half is the ability to dynamically set attributes on an object in much the same manner that we can retrieve them. Normally, we would change the name attribute on an Recipe object by calling the setter method:

```
Recipe *myRecipe = ...
[myRecipe setName:@"Yummy Cookies"];
```

Like the earlier getter accessor, this requires preexisting knowledge of the Recipe object to be able to use that accessor without compiler warnings. However, with KVC, we can access it in a more dynamic manner:

```
id myRecipe = ...
[myRecipe setValue:@"Yummy Cookies" forKey:@"name"];
```

This call will attempt to use the setter -setName: if it is available; if it is not, then it will look for and use the attribute directly if it is available, and failing that, it will call -setValue:forUndefinedKey: on the target object. The combination of the dynamic getter coupled with the dynamic setter allows us to manipulate objects without having to write accessors and without having to know (or care!) if they exist. This is used to great effect in one of the Core Data recipes to create a preferences singleton object that reads its values from a properties table. See Chapter 12, *Recipe: Dynamic Parameters*, on page 225.

@property

In addition, as of OS X 10.5 Leopard, we have the new keyword @property that allows us to synthesize accessors to attributes on an object. This new feature plays very nicely with KVC, and the two can be used together to produce extremely dynamic and flexible code. By utilizing the new @property keyword, we can instruct the compiler to generate getter and setter accessors for us that are KVO compliant. In a 32-bit application, we can define a @property that has the same object type and name as a defined ivar. This will tell the compiler that getter and setter accessors exist or will exist for that ivar. In a 64-bit application, the ivar itself is not required because the property definition handles that for us as well. For example, if we had an object with the following header:

```
@interface MyObject : NSObject
{
    NSString *myString;
}

@property (retain) NSString *myString;
@end
```

Xcode would interpret it the same as the following header:

```
@interface MyObject : NSObject
{
  NSString *myString;
}

- (NSString*)myString;
- (void)setMyString:(NSString*)string;

@end
```

In combination with the @property keyword, we have the @synthesize and @dynamic keywords for use in our implementation files. @synthesize will generate the actual accessors that the @property alludes to in the header. Therefore, in our example MyObject.m file, we can declare the following:

```
#import "MyObject.h"

@implementation MyObject

@synthesize myString;

@end
```

and have the same effective code as this:

```
#import "MyObject.h"

@implementation MyObject

- (NSString*)myString;
{
  return myString;
}
```

```
- (void)setMyString:(NSString*)string;
{
  @synchronized(self) {
    if ([string isEqualToString:myString]) return;
    [myString release];
    myString = [string retain];
  }
}

@end
```

The retain in the setter is added by the compiler because we specified it in the property. If we had set it to assign instead, then no retain would have occurred. Likewise, the locking of the ivar is a default option that we could have turned off by adding the nonatomic option to the property definition.

When dealing with multiple properties on an object, this can be a great time-saver. There have also been indications that the accessors generated by the compiler are faster than the "normal" accessors that developers write. In addition to generating accessors, the @synthesize keyword is smart about what it implements. If we need to implement our own setter for a property, then it will not overwrite that setter.

Alongside the @synthesize property, we have the @dynamic property. Unlike @synthesize, which generates the accessors for us, @dynamic tells the compiler that while the accessors for the property are not there at compile time, they will be there at run time and to not produce a warning for them. @synthesize and @dynamic are sibling keywords. For each property, we can use one or the other but not both.[3] If the accessor methods will be implemented at runtime, we would use the @dynamic property instead of the @synthesize property so that the compiler does not produce a warning. This is particularly useful for Core Data subclasses, which we will discuss in Chapter 4, *Under the Hood of Core Data*, on page 45.

It should be noted that it is possible to have a @property definition that does not match the name of the ivar. For example, it is fairly common to have ivars that start with an underscore, but the accessors do not include the underscore. The @property can handle this as well as part of the @synthesize and @dynamic calls.

---

3. However, neither is required in a situation where we are implementing the accessors ourselves.

```objc
@interface MyObject : NSObject
{
  NSString *_myString;
}

@property (retain) NSString *myString;

@end

@implementation MyObject

@synthesize myString = _myString;

@end
```

3.2 Key Value Observing

Key Value Observing (KVO) is the sister API to KVC. KVO allows us to request notifications when an attribute has changed. By observing attributes on an object, we can react when those attributes are changed. KVO is also implemented via an informal protocol on the NSObject, and you register and remove observers using -addObserver:forKeyPath:options:context: and -removeObserver:forKeyPath:. Although, like KVC, there are other methods involved in the protocol, these are the primary two used.

If we wanted to observe the name value on a recipe, we would add ourselves (or another object) as an observer for that value like this:

```objc
static NSString *kPragProgObserver = @"PragProgObserver"
id myRecipe = ...
[myRecipe addObserver:self
        forKeyPath:@"name"
            options:(NSKeyValueObservingOptionNew|NSKeyValueObservingOptionOld)
            context:kPragProgObserver];
```

What this snippet of code is doing is adding self as an observer to the myRecipe object and asking that when the name value changes to please notify self of that change and include both the old value and the new value in that notification. We pass along a context so that we can ensure we are acting on observations meant only for us and that they are not accidentally intercepted. After this code has been called, any time the name property is changed on *that instance of Recipe*, the -observeValueForKeyPath:ofObject:change:context: is called upon self.

We can then handle that change notification as appropriate:

```
- (void)observeValueForKeyPath:(NSString*)keyPath
                    ofObject:(id)object
                      change:(NSDictionary*)change
                     context:(void*)context
{
  if (context != kPragProgObserver) {
    [super observeValueForKeyPath:keyPath
                    ofObject:object
                      change:change
                     context:context];
    return;
  }
  NSLog(@"Attribute %@ changed from %@ to %@", keyPath,
    [change valueForKey:NSKeyValueChangeOldKey],
    [change valueForKey:NSKeyValueChangeNewKey]);
}
```

When the variable is changed, we will see output similar to the following:

```
Attribute name changed from untitled to Beef Chili
```

When we are done observing a value, we can stop receiving messages by passing -removeObserver:forKeyPath: to the observed object:

```
id myRecipe = ...
[myRecipe removeObserver:self
            forKeyPath:@"name"];
```

KVO is what allows views to automatically refresh themselves from the model when the data has changed. When a view is initialized, it uses KVO to connect all its components to the underlying objects and uses the notifications to refresh itself.

3.3 Cocoa Bindings and Core Data

The combination of KVO/KVC (collectively referred to as Cocoa Bindings) and Core Data reduces the amount of code that we are required to write by a considerable amount. In the previous chapter, we wrote almost no code to create and display our recipe objects. Nearly all the work that we did was in Interface Builder. In this section, we will discuss each of those interface objects that we used and how they worked with Core Data.

How does this apply to our application? Let's review the user interface that we built in Chapter 2, *Getting Started with Core Data*, on page 7 and how we used KVO and KVC.

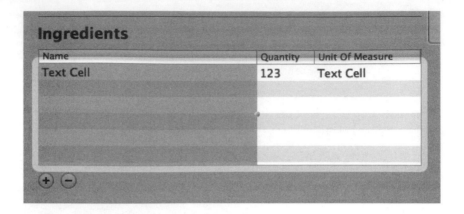

Figure 3.1: SELECT EACH NSTABLECOLUMN INDIVIDUALLY.

NSTableView

In our recipe application, we make heavy use of the NSTableView. In the main window of our application, we have two table views, one to list all of the recipes and another to list the ingredients for those recipes. Whenever an application needs to display a list of items or a grid of data, the NSTableView is the element to use.

NSTableView, like NSOutlineView (as discussed in Section 3.4, *NSOutline-View*, on page 39), plays very nicely with Core Data. This is especially true when the NSTableView is backed by an NSArrayController that is feeding the data. However, it is possible to use NSTableView with a custom data source if that is appropriate for the problem at hand. However, when bound with an NSArrayController, then the NSTableView can be manipulated with other objects such as the NSSearchView discussed in a moment to produce interfaces that integrate smoothly and give a great user experience.

In an NSTableView, like the NSOutlineView, we do not actually bind the table itself to the NSArrayController. Instead, we select each column individually and bind it to a property of the objects in the NSArrayController (see Figure 3.1). As we did in Chapter 2, *Getting Started with Core Data*, on page 7, we bind the column to the arrangedObjects controller key and the model key path to the value we want displayed in that column, as shown in Figure 3.2, on the facing page.

Figure 3.2: BIND THE TABLE COLUMN TO THE CORE DATA PROPERTY.

With this configuration, the NSTableView will display the data from the NSArrayController automatically and, thanks to KVO, will stay in sync with the data stored in the persistence layer.

NSArrayController

NSArrayController is an extremely useful object when working with Core Data because it is aware of the Core Data layer and knows how to talk to it without any additional code on our part. When we configure it within Interface Builder, all that we really need to give it is the NSManagedObjectContext and a data object type. The rest of the work—retrieving the objects, updating those objects, and creating new ones—is all handled for us.

NSArrayController also understands relationships between objects when it is working with Core Data. In our recipe application, we have one NSArrayController configured to manage RecipeIngredient objects. Based on our data model, these are child objects that are bound to a specific recipe. Because NSArrayController understands these relationships, we can configure it to pull and display only those RecipeIngredient objects that are connected to a Recipe object that is selected in another NSArray-Controller. This again is made possible by KVC and KVO. When we configure the RecipeIngredient's NSArrayController to provide only those ingredients that are related to the specific recipe, what it is doing behind the scenes is accessing the Recipe object and requesting its ingredients property via KVC. In the RecipeIngredient's NSArrayController, we bind the NSManagedObjectContext so that new ingredients can be added. In addition to properly being able to create (and remove) objects from the persistence layer, the NSArrayController will also manage the relationship between the newly created or removed RecipeIngredient and the parent Recipe object.

All of this works because Core Data is the entire persistence layer and is accessed in a consistent way no matter what object is being dealt with. Because Core Data uses KVO and KVC, our controller objects do not need to know very much about the objects, other than the name of the objects and where they are stored. The rest is all resolved at runtime based on the settings that we provide in Interface Builder. In our recipe application, we have one NSArrayController that is bound to the Recipe entity in Core Data. Because we also bound that NSArrayController to our NSManagedObjectContext, it is able to retrieve those Recipe entities automatically and make them available to the rest of the user interface. When our interface is loaded, those NSArrayController objects go out to that NSManagedObjectContext and ask for the entities that currently exist. Once they are loaded into the NSArrayController objects, any view element associated with them will be notified, via KVO, that the data is available for display. All of this happens behind the scenes without requiring us to write code for any of this.

NSFormatter

Users expect fields in the interface to accept their input and format it appropriately. This is where NSFormatter objects come into play. When dealing with any type of number, it is best to add an NSNumberFormatter to the text field or table column and define its display. Likewise, when working with dates, use an NSDateFormatter on the field or column to ensure that the data will be formatted and validated correctly before it is stored in the Core Data repository. When working with Core Data, it is sometimes necessary to manipulate the display of the data both so that the user's input can be validated and so that it can be displayed in a usable form. For instance, it is not a very good user experience to display currency as 3.99 rather than $3.99 or to display a date in raw seconds.

In our application, we used an NSNumberFormatter to display the quantity in the ingredients column of our second NSTableView. If we were to add a shopping list to our application, we would also use NSNumberFormatter objects to display currency and NSDateFormatter objects to show date and time information.

To add an NSFormatter to a field (either a column or a text field), select it in the library palette, and drag it onto the interface element. Once it is in place, you can configure its details in the Attributes inspector, as shown in Figure 3.3, on the next page. The Attributes inspector will allow you to configure exactly how the data is presented to the user.

In addition to properly displaying number and date data, the NSFormatter classes will also accept input from the user and send it back to the model in the correct format. For example, by applying NSNumberFormatter to the quantity column of the ingredients table, we are guaranteed to receive an NSNumber back from the user interface.

Once an NSFormatter has been applied to an object, it can be a little tricky to reference it again to make changes. To be able to change or remove an NSFormatter once it has been applied, you can select the user interface element, and a small double bracket icon will appear below it. Selecting that icon will reference the NSFormatter again so that it can be manipulated. See Figure 3.4, on page 39.

3.4 Other Interface Elements That Use KVO, KVC, and Core Data

Although the previous list shows how we are using KVO and KVC to access our Core Data repository in our recipe application, we should quickly review the other elements that, if we wanted or needed to, could be utilized to display the data in our application as well.

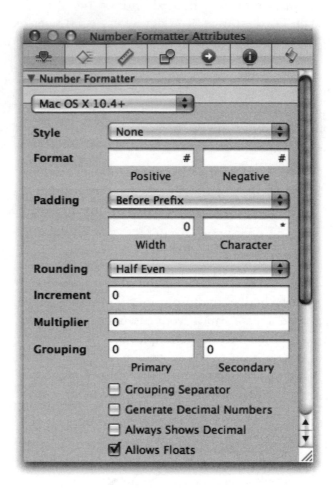

Figure 3.3: NSNumberFormatter Attributes inspector

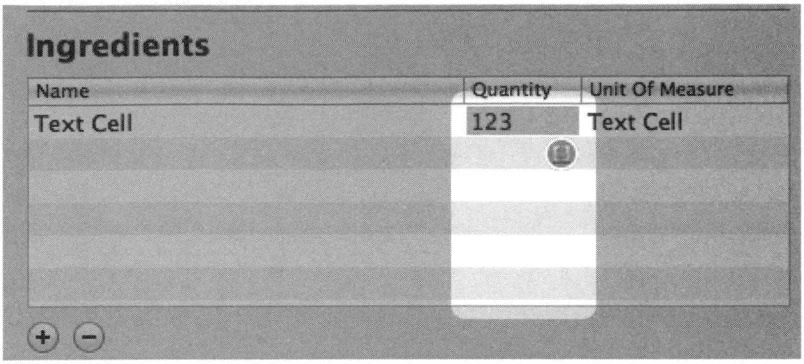

Figure 3.4: ACCESSING AN EXISTING NSFORMATTER ON AN ELEMENT

NSObjectController

NSObjectController shares a lot of similarities with the NSArrayController discussed earlier. However, unlike the NSArrayController, the NSObject-Controller is designed to represent one instance rather than an array of instances. One common usage of the NSObjectController is to represent the selected object of an NSArrayController, thereby making it clearer as to what data is being displayed in the interface elements that are bound to the NSObjectController as opposed to an NSArrayController. Another common usage is to have an entire interface, such as a detail sheet or child window, be bound to the values within an NSObjectController and then have the File's Owner reference and populate that NSObjectController. In this design, the File's Owner (usually a subclass of NSWindowController) simply has to populate the NSObjectController with a call to -setContent:, and the entire UI will get populated automatically. This again makes the maintenance of the code very easy and also improves readability.

NSOutlineView

If we wanted to change the look of our application, we could display a single NSOutlineView instead of the two table views we have currently. With an NSOutlineView, we could display a list of recipes with a hierarchy of ingredients listed under them, as depicted in Figure 3.5, on the next page.

NSOutlineView shares a lot in common with the NSTableView object. In fact, it is a subclass of NSTableView. The major difference is that the NSOutlineView displays data in both a column format as well as a hier-

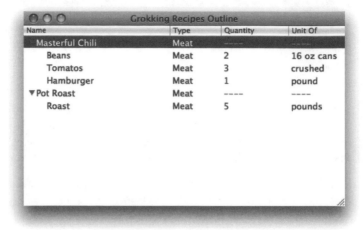

Figure 3.5: OUTLINE VIEW OF RECIPES

archal format. This changes how the data needs to be represented and accessed. Instead of a flat array of objects, the NSOutlineView expects the data to be in a tree structure. Fortunately, there is a controller designed just for that use: NSTreeController. Some care needs to be taken when working with Core Data and an NSOutlineView. In general, the NSOutlineView and the NSTreeController expect the data to be in a fairly organized state. NSTreeController expects each parent (or branch) to have children accessible via the same methods. This is a bit counterintuitive to having descriptive names for relationships between objects, and I normally implement accessors instead of making my relationships generic. For instance, if we had a recipe that has children named RecipeIngredients, I would add another accessor to that relationship called children, purely for the NSOutlineView to use. We will discuss custom NSManagedObject classes in the next chapter.

Unlike its parent object, NSTableView, the NSOutlineView does not work as cleanly as you might expect. You can combine it with the NSTreeController, but you get a lot more functionality and control by implementing the data source protocol for the NSOutlineView instead of using the NSTreeController object. Since we have seen continual improvement in the last couple of releases of OS X on the NSTreeController, I suspect this situation will change in the future. However, for now, the data source protocol is the better option when working with the NSOutlineView object.

NSTreeController

As discussed in Section 3.4, *NSOutlineView*, on page 39, NSTreeController objects are primarily used by the NSOutlineView interface element. Although they can store any data that lends itself to a tree structure, they are best suited as a controller for NSOutlineView objects. Unfortunately, there is still quite a bit of work to be done with the NSTreeController, and the results we get from working with it can be unexpected and unclear. Therefore, I recommend skipping it at this time and implementing the data source protocol instead when working with tree data.

NSSearchField

The NSSearchField interface element is an extremely useful tool to provide that extra little bit of polish to an interface. Its primary purpose is to filter the objects in an NSArrayController. This does not seem like much until we remember that, thanks to KVO, any tables or interface elements associated with that NSArrayController will get updated automatically and instantly. This means if we put a search field into our application and link it to our NSArrayController of Recipe objects, our source list of recipes will automatically be filtered based on the user input into that NSSearchField. Even better, we don't have to write any code to accomplish this! All that we need to do to implement it is configure the bindings for the NSSearchField.

To accomplish this, first we need to add an NSSearchField to our application. In Figure 3.6, on the next page, we have decreased the vertical size of the Recipe source list and inserted an NSSearchField above it. Next we need to configure its bindings.

As shown in Figure 3.7, on page 43, the NSSearchField interface element works with an NSPredicate. We write the predicate in the Predicate Format field substituting $value for whatever the user inputs into the search field and using the controller key, model key path, and value transformer to bind it to our data. In this example, we want to filter on the name of recipes; therefore, we bind this NSSearchField to our recipe's NSArrayController using the controller key of filterPredicate and a model key path of name.

Once we add one predicate, another will appear on the Bindings tab for the NSSearchField. This is intended so that we can use a search field

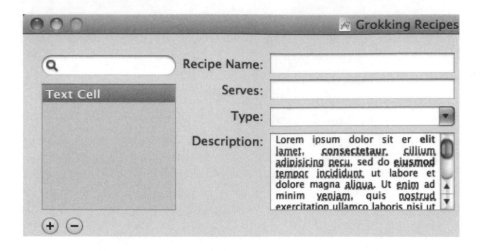

Figure 3.6: ADDING AN NSSEARCHFIELD TO OUR APPLICATION

for more than one type of search. Each search will be shown in the drop-down on the NSSearchField, and the Display Name binding will be shown to the user. This allows us to create one NSSearchField that can search for recipe names, ingredients, descriptions, or anything else we may need.

Once the binding is complete, we are done adding a basic search field. Running the application will show that text entered into the search field impacts the list of recipes, as shown in Figure 3.8, on the next page.

Now that we have a better understanding of the user interface we built in Chapter 2, *Getting Started with Core Data*, on page 7, we can next look at the structure of the Core Data code provided for us in the template to get a firm understanding both of it and of how to improve it.

Figure 3.7: NSSEARCHFIELD BINDINGS

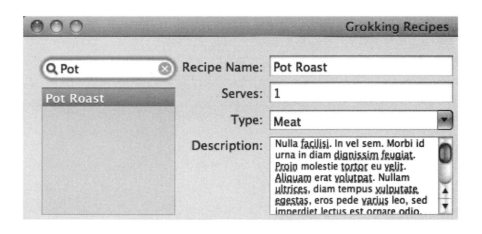

Figure 3.8: SEARCH FILTER RUNNING AGAINST THE RECIPE LIST

Chapter 4

Under the Hood of Core Data

The more we understand the details of Core Data, the better equipped we are to understand when something goes wrong or how to accomplish a task that is off the beaten path.

In my experience of working with and writing persistence layers for various languages, I am constantly amazed at how simple and elegant the Core Data API is. There is very little overlap in functionality between the individual pieces of Core Data—no wasted space or unnecessary redundancy. Because Core Data is built upon the infrastructure of Objective-C and Core Foundation, it does not seek to duplicate functionality that already exists in other parts of the overall API but instead uses it to its full extent.

In this chapter, we will walk through the various pieces that make up Core Data and explore how they apply to the ways that we use Core Data and how they apply to the application we are developing in this book. By the end of this chapter, we will have a firmer grasp of what Core Data is, what we can do with it, and how to use it to its full capabilities.

The Core Data API, or *stack* as it is commonly called, consists of three primary pieces: NSPersistentStoreCoordinator, NSManagedObjectModel, and NSManagedObjectContext. All of these work together to allow a program to retrieve and store NSManagedObject objects. In most situations, the program will access NSManagedObjectContext only once the stack has been created. It is possible to access the other components of the stack, but it is rarely necessary.

Joe Asks...

What Is a Stack?

The term *stack* has a few different meanings depending on its context. In this context, it refers to a multilayered structure that passes data around in a vertical manner. Vertical here means coming in through the top layer and reaching down to the last, or bottom, layer. Data is never passed directly to the bottom layer or any of the middle layers; it always accessed from the top.

4.1 NSManagedObject

NSManagedObject is the object we work with the most in a Core Data application. Each instance of NSManagedObject represents one entity in our Core Data repository. By combining Core Data with KVC and KVO, this one object can dynamically represent any object that we need and that can be defined in our data model.

All of the properties and relationships defined in our data model are available and are easy to access directly from the NSManagedObject. Without subclassing it, we can access values associated with an NSManagedObject in the following ways.

Accessing Attributes

Attributes are the easiest to access. By utilizing KVC, we can get or set any attribute on the NSManagedObject directly. You may have noticed that we did not write a Recipe entity in the previous chapter. At this point in our application, NSManagedObject provides all the functionality that we require. For example, we could get the name as follows:

```
NSManagedObject *recipe = ...;
NSString *name = [recipe valueForKey:@"name"];
```

Likewise, we can set the name in a similar fashion:

```
NSManagedObject *recipe = ...;
[recipe setValue:@"New Name" forKey:@"name"];
```

When we want to subclass NSManagedObject, we can also define properties for the attributes (and relationships discussed in a moment) so that we can access them directly. In the header of our subclass, we would define the properties normally:

`Spotlight/PPRecipe.h`

```
@interface PPRecipe : NSManagedObject {

}

@property (assign) NSString *desc;
@property (assign) NSString *name;
@property (assign) NSString *type;
@property (assign) NSManagedObject *author;
@property (assign) NSDate *lastUsed;
```

As you can see, we are defining the property like normal, but there are no ivars associated with those properties. Since these properties are created dynamically at runtime, we do not need to declare them in the header. However, we do need to flag them as dynamic so that the compiler will not issue a warning. This is done in the implementation file:

`Spotlight/PPRecipe.m`

```
@implementation PPRecipe

@dynamic desc;
@dynamic name;
@dynamic type;
@dynamic author;
@dynamic lastUsed;
```

By declaring them as @dynamic, we are telling the compiler to ignore any warnings associated with these properties because we "promise" to generate them at runtime. Naturally, if they turn up missing at runtime, then our application is going to crash. However, when we are working with NSManagedObject objects, the attributes will be looked up for us, and we do not need to implement anything. By adding that code, we can access the attribute directly, as shown in the following example:

```
PPRecipe *myRecipe = ...;
NSString *recipeName = [myRecipe name];
//Do something with the name
[myRecipe setName:recipeName];
```

Primitive Access

It should be noted that accessing the attribute via KVC or properties will trigger KVO notifications that the attribute has changed. There are situations where we do not want this to occur or where we prefer it to occur later. In those situations, we can access the attribute using the -primitiveValueForKey: and -setPrimitiveValue:forKey: methods. Both of these methods work the same as the -valueForKey: and -setValue:forKey methods that we are used to working with, but they do not cause KVO notifications to fire. This means that the rest of our application will be unaware of any changes we make until and unless we notify it.

Where is this useful? I find it quite useful when I am loading in data from an external source and the data is going to impact several attributes at once. Imagine we wrote a recipe importer that accepted a comma-separated value (CSV) file from another recipe application. In that situation, we may not want the UI or other parts of our application making decisions based on the data in the middle of the import. Therefore, we would want to update the values without notifications, and once all of them are done, we let the notifications go out. The code to handle this situation would look something like this:

```
- (void)importData:(NSDictionary*)values //CSV translated into a dictionary
{
  [self willChangeValueForKey:@"name"];
  [self willChangeValueForKey:@"desc"];
  [self willChangeValueForKey:@"serves"];
  [self willChangeValueForKey:@"type"];
  [self setPrimitiveValue:[values valueForKey:@"name"] forKey:@"name"];
  [self setPrimitiveValue:[values valueForKey:@"desc"] forKey:@"desc"];
  [self setPrimitiveValue:[values valueForKey:@"serves"] forKey:@"serves"];
  [self setPrimitiveValue:[values valueForKey:@"type"] forKey:@"type"];
  [self didChangeValueForKey:@"type"];
  [self didChangeValueForKey:@"serves"];
  [self didChangeValueForKey:@"desc"];
  [self didChangeValueForKey:@"name"];
}
```

In this example code, we are handling all the change notifications ourselves and setting the values into our NSManagedObject directly using the -setPrimitiveValue:forKey: method. This will cause all the values to be updated prior to the notifications being fired.

Accessing Relationships

Accessing relationships on an NSManagedObject is nearly as easy as accessing attributes. There is a bit of a difference between working with a to-one relationship and a to-many relationship, though.

Accessing a To-One Relationship

When we are accessing a to-one relationship, we can treat it the same as an attribute. For example, the relationship between Recipe and RecipeIngredient is a to-one relationship from the RecipeIngredient side. Therefore, if we were accessing this relationship from that point of view, the code would be as follows:

```
NSManagedObject *ingredient = ...;
NSManagedObject *recipe = [ingredient valueForKey:@"recipe"];
```

In this example, we are using the -valueForKey: KVC method to access the relationship, and the NSManagedObject will return the object on the other side of the relationship, the Recipe entity. Likewise, to set the recipe for a RecipeIngredient, we would use the following code:

```
NSManagedObject *ingredient = ...;
NSManagedObject *recipe = ...;
[ingredient setValue:recipe forKey:@"recipe"];
```

Accessing a To-Many Relationship

The many side of a relationship is stored orderless. What this means is that each time we fetch the objects on the many side of a relationship, the order is not guaranteed, and it is probable that the order will change between fetches. However, we are guaranteed that each object will be included only once. In other words, when we access a to-many relationship using KVC, we will get an NSSet back. For example, if we want to access the ingredients of a recipe, we would use code similar to the following:

```
NSManagedObject *recipe = ...;
NSSet *ingredients = [recipe valueForKey:@"ingredients"];
```

Likewise, setting the ingredients into a recipe is as follows:

```
NSManagedObject *recipe = ...;
NSSet *someIngredients = ...;
[recipe setValue:someIngredients forKey:@"ingredients"];
```

Mutable Access of To-Many Relationships

You might note that the NSSet we get back when accessing a to-many relationship is immutable. Adding an object to a to-many relationship with a immutable NSSet would require creating a mutable copy of the NSSet, adding the new object to the NSMutableSet and then setting the NSMutableSet back onto the parent object. That's painful and fortunately unnecessary. When we want to add an object to a to-many relationship, we can use -mutableSetValueForKey: in the place of -valueForKey:. This will return an NSMutableSet for us that is already associated with the parent object and reduces our code to the following:

```
NSManagedObject *newIngredient = ...;
NSManagedObject *recipe = ...;
NSMutableSet *ingredients = [recipe mutableSetValueForKey:@"ingredients"];
[ingredients addObject:newIngredient];
```

Note that we did not need to set the NSMutableSet back into the Recipe entity, and therefore the code to add an object to a to-many relationship is quite short.

One important thing to notice in these relationship examples is that when we are updating the relationship, we are updating only one side of it. Because we defined these relationships as double-sided (that is, it includes an inverse relationship that we defined in Section 2.5, *Building the Data Model*, on page 9), Core Data handles keeping the integrity of the relationship intact. When we update one side of the relationship, Core Data automatically goes in and sets the other side for us.

Primitive Access

Like accessing attributes discussed earlier, changes to a relationship will fire KVO notifications. Since there are situations where we would not want this to occur or where we would want a finer-grained control over the notifications, there are primitive accessors for relationships as well. However, there is no primitive method for retrieving an NSMutable-Set for a to-many relationship. Therefore, if the code requires changes to a relationship with either delayed or no observations being fired, then we would need to use -primitiveValueForKey: to get back an NSSet, call -mutableCopy on the NSSet, add our new object to the NSMutableSet, and finally use -setPrimitiveValue:forKey: to apply the changes.

Property Accessors

Relationships can use properties just like attributes discussed earlier. In the code in Section 4.1, *Mutable Access of To-Many Relationships*, on the preceding page, if we wanted to add a property to retrieve the RecipeIngredient relationship, we would declare the following property:

```
@property (retain) NSSet *recipeIngredients;
```

And then flag it as dynamic in the implementation file.

Subclassing NSManagedObject

Although NSManagedObject provides a tremendous amount of flexibility and handles the majority of the work a data object normally does, it does not cover every possibility, and there are occasions where we would want to subclass it. Subclassing to gain @property access to attributes and relationships is one common situation, but we may also want to add other convenience methods or additional functionality to the object. When this arises, there are some general rules to remember.

Methods That Are Not Safe to Override

In Apple's documentation, the following methods should never be overridden:

-primitiveValueForKey:, -setPrimitiveValue:forKey:, -isEqual:, -hash, -superclass, -class, -self, -zone, -isProxy:, -isKindOfClass:, -isMemberOfClass:, -conformsToProtocol:, -respondsToSelector:, -retain, -release, -autorelease, -retainCount, -managedObjectContext, -entity, -objectID, -isInserted, -isUpdated, -isDeleted, -isFault, -alloc, -allocWithZone:, +new, +instancesRespondToSelector:, +instanceMethodForSelector:, -methodForSelector:, -methodSignatureForSelector:, and -isSubclassOfClass:.

That's quite a list! Most, if not all, of these are common sense, and experience with Objective-C explains why these should not be overridden. Even though this is a fairly long list, I would add a few more.

-initXXX. There is really no reason or benefit to overriding the -init methods of an NSManagedObject, and there are situations where doing so will have unpredictable results. Although it is not specifically against the documentation to override the -init methods, I recommend strongly against it. The -awakeFromInsert and -awakeFromFetch methods provide sufficient access that overriding -init is unnecessary. Both -awakeFromInsert and -awakeFromFetch are discussed in more depth later in this chapter.

All of the KVO methods. The documentation flags these methods as "discouraged," but I would put them in the "do not subclass" list. Again, there is no reason to override these methods, and any logic that you would want to put into them can probably be put somewhere else with fewer issues.

-description. The -description method is used in logging fairly often. It is a great way to dump the contents of an object out to the logs during debugging. However, when we are dealing with faults (discussed in

Chapter 6, *Performance Tuning*, on page 91), we do not want to fire a fault in the -description method. Since the default implementation of -description does the right thing with regard to faults, it is best that we not try to override its behavior.

-dealloc is normally the place that we release memory before the object is being freed. However, when we are dealing with NSManagedObject objects, it is possible that the object will not actually be released from memory when we think it will. In fact, the -dealloc method may never get called in the life cycle of our application! Instead of releasing objects in the -dealloc method, it is recommended that we use -didTurnIntoFault as our point of releasing transient resources. -didTurnIntoFault will be called whenever the NSManagedObject is "faulted," which occurs far more often than the object actually being removed from memory.

-finalize is on the list for the same reason as -dealloc. When dealing with NSManagedObject objects, -finalize is not the proper point to be releasing resources.

Methods to Override

With the long list of methods that we should not override, what methods should we consider overriding? There are a few where it is common to override them.

-didTurnIntoFault

This method is called after the NSManagedObject has been turned into a fault. It is a good place to release transient resources. One important thing to note is that when this method is called, all the stored values/relationships in the NSManagedObject are already out of memory. If you access any of them, it will fire the fault and pull them all back into memory again.

-willTurnIntoFault

Similar to -didTurnIntoFault, this method is called just before the NSManagedObject is turned into a fault. If your code needs to access attributes or relationships on the NSManagedObject before it is turned into a fault, then this is the entry point to use. Transient resources that impact attributes and relationships should be released here.

-awakeFromInsert

As mentioned, overriding any of the -init methods is risky and unnecessary. However, it is very useful to be able to prepare an NSManagedObject before it starts accepting data. Perhaps we want to set up some logical defaults or assign some relationships before handing the object to the user. In these situations, we use -awakeFromInsert. As the name implies, this method is called right after the NSManagedObject is created from an insert call. This method is called before any values are set and is a perfect opportunity to set default values, initialize transient properties, and perform other tasks that we would normally handle in the -init method. This method is called exactly once in the entire lifetime of an object. It will not be called on the next execution of the application, and it will not be called when an object is read in from the persistent store. Therefore, we do not need to worry about overriding values that have been set previously. When we override this method, we should be sure to call (super awakeFromInsert) at the very beginning of our implementation to allow the NSManagedObject to finish anything it needs to before we begin our code.

-awakeFromFetch

-awakeFromFetch is the counterpart to -awakeFromInsert. The -awakeFromFetch method will be called every time the object is retrieved from the persistent store (that is, loaded from disk). This method is highly useful for setting up transient objects or connections that the NSManagedObject will use during its life cycle. Because this method is called before the data is loaded into the NSManagedObject, care should be taken to not access or change any relationships that are associated with the NSManagedObject. Like the -awakeFromInsert method, when we override this method, we should call (super awakeFromFetch); before any of our own code is called.

4.2 NSFetchRequest

NSFetchRequest is the part of Core Data that causes people to think it is a database API instead of an object hierarchy. Whenever we want to retrieve objects from Core Data, we will normally use an NSFetchRequest to do the retrieval. There are two parts to the creation of an NSFetchRequest: setting the entity to be retrieved and optionally defining an NSPredicate to filter the objects we want retrieved.

Setting the Entity

The one thing that we must do as part of every NSFetchRequest is define what entity we want returned from the fetch. We do this by passing the appropriate NSEntityDescription to the NSFetchRequest. For example, if we wanted to retrieve recipe entities, we would construct the NSFetchRequest as follows:

```
NSManagedObjectContext *moc = [self managedObjectContext];
NSFetchRequest *request = [[NSFetchRequest alloc] init];
[request setEntity:[NSEntityDescription entityForName:@"Recipe"
                               inManagedObjectContext:moc]];
```

In this example code, we are constructing a new NSFetchRequest and calling -setEntity: on it. We are using the class method +entityForName:in-ManagedObjectContext: on the NSEntityDescription class to get the appropriate instance of NSEntityDescription back for the setter.

Executing a Fetch Request

Once we have constructed our NSFetchRequest, we need to execute it against the NSManagedObjectContext to get back the results. Like a result set when accessing a database, an executed NSFetchRequest will return an NSArray of entities that match our search criteria. Since it is possible that a search will fail, the execution of an NSFetchRequest accepts a pointer to an NSError to describe any problems that resulted from the execution. For example, if we wanted to execute the fetch from the previous example, we could use the following code:

```
NSManagedObjectContext *moc = [self managedObjectContext];
NSFetchRequest *request = [[NSFetchRequest alloc] init];
[request setEntity:[NSEntityDescription entityForName:@"Recipe"
                               inManagedObjectContext:moc]];
NSError *error = nil;
NSArray *results = [moc executeFetchRequest:request error:&error];
if (error) {
  [NSApp presentError:error];
  return;
}
```

In this example, we are calling -executeFetchRequest:error: on the NSManagedObjectContext, passing in the NSFetchRequest and a pointer to a local NSError. If the fetch failed with an error, then the pointer will be directed to an instance of NSError that describes the problem, and the NSArray will be assigned to nil. In that situation, we ask the NSApplication to present the error for us and return. If there is no error, then we can proceed with our code. Note that the NSArray is guaranteed to not be nil at this point, but it could be empty if no results are returned.

NSPredicate

When we don't want every instance of an entity returned, we then use an NSPredicate to narrow the search or filter the results. The NSPredicate class is quite complex and powerful and can be used for more things than just Core Data. It is frequently used to filter the results of an NSArray by acting on the KVC API and doing logic checks on the objects contained in the NSArray.

One of the most common ways to use an NSPredicate is to construct a SQL-like query such as the following example:

```
NSManagedObjectContext *moc = [self managedObjectContext];
NSFetchRequest *request = [[NSFetchRequest alloc] init];
[request setEntity:[NSEntityDescription entityForName:@"Recipe"
                               inManagedObjectContext:moc]];
NSPredicate *predicate = [NSPredicate predicateWithFormat:@"serves > 10"];
[request setPredicate:predicate];
```

There are many different ways to build an NSPredicate. The one shown in the previous example accepts a SQL-like NSString and can accept any number of parameters after the NSString. For example, if we were going to pass in the number of servings, we would rewrite the NSPredicate as follows:

```
NSUInteger numberOfServings = 10;
NSManagedObjectContext *moc = [self managedObjectContext];
NSFetchRequest *request = [[NSFetchRequest alloc] init];
[request setEntity:[NSEntityDescription entityForName:@"Recipe"
                               inManagedObjectContext:moc]];
NSPredicate *predicate = nil;
predicate = [NSPredicate predicateWithFormat:@"serves > %i", numberOfServings];
[request setPredicate:predicate];
```

It is possible to add as many parameters to the NSPredicate as needed.

The NSPredicate class is quite flexible and can be used in a large number of ways. For further reading on how to use the NSPredicate class to its full potential, I recommend Apple's *Predicate Programming Guide*.[1]

Stored Fetch Requests

In addition to constructing the NSFetchRequest directly in code, it is possible to build them within the data model and store them for later

---

1. http://developer.apple.com/documentation/Cocoa/Conceptual/Predicates/Articles/pUsing.html

Figure 4.1: STORED FETCH REQUEST

use. By storing the fetch requests within the model itself, it is possible for us to change them as needed without having to go through all the code looking for every place that it is used. Simply changing it in the model will automatically update wherever it is being used. To store an NSFetchRequest within the data model, we select the entity that we want to run the request against and choose Design > Data Model > Add Fetch Request from the main menu. From there we will be able to set the name of the fetch request and define its predicate, as shown in Figure 4.1.

Once we have the fetch request in our data model, we can request a reference to it by asking the NSManagedObjectModel. Once we have a reference to the NSFetchRequest, we can execute it in the same manner as we do with an NSFetchRequest that has been constructed in code.

GrokkingRecipes_v1/AppDelegate.m

```objc
- (NSArray*)retrieveBigMeals
{
  NSManagedObjectContext *moc = [self managedObjectContext];
  NSManagedObjectModel *mom = [self managedObjectModel];
  NSFetchRequest *request = [mom fetchRequestTemplateForName:@"bigMeals"];
  NSError *error = nil;
  NSArray *result = [moc executeFetchRequest:request error:&error];
  if (error) {
    [NSApp presentError:error];
    return nil;
  }
  return result;
}
```

As shown, we call the -fetchRequestTemplateForName: method on the NSManagedObjectModel, which will return a fully formed NSFetchRequest to us. This NSFetchRequest will already have the NSEntityDescription and NSPredicate set so that we can execute the NSFetchRequest immediately.

4.3 NSSortDescriptor

NSSortDescriptor has been around longer than Core Data has; however, it is quite useful for ordering data. As mentioned previously, data that comes from a to-many relationship is unordered by default, and it is up to us to order it. For example, if we wanted to retrieve all the recipes and then sort them by their name property in alphabetical order, this would require an additional step as part of the fetch.

`GrokkingRecipes_v1/AppDelegate.m`

```
- (NSArray*)allRecipesSortedByName
{
  NSSortDescriptor *nameSort = [[NSSortDescriptor alloc] initWithKey:@"name"
                                                  ascending:YES];
  NSArray *sorters = [NSArray arrayWithObject:nameSort];
  [nameSort release], nameSort = nil;

  NSManagedObjectContext *moc = [self managedObjectContext];
  NSFetchRequest *request = [[NSFetchRequest alloc] init];
  [request setSortDescriptors:sorters];
  [request setEntity:[NSEntityDescription entityForName:@"Recipe"
                            inManagedObjectContext:moc]];
  NSError *error = nil;
  NSArray *result = [moc executeFetchRequest:request
                                  error:&error];
  [request release], request = nil;
  if (error) {
    [NSApp presentError:error];
    return nil;
  }
  return [result sortedArrayUsingDescriptors:sorters];
}
```

In this example, we are retrieving all the recipe entities by creating an NSFetchRequest with the NSEntityDescription set to our Recipe entity and no predicate. However, in addition to fetching the recipe entities, we also want them sorted. We can accomplish this by adding an NSArray of NSSortDescriptor instances directly to the NSFetchRequest, which will cause the returned NSArray to be properly sorted.

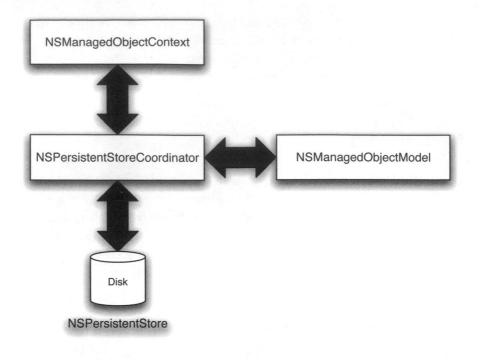

Figure 4.2: The Core Data stack

The NSSortDescriptor takes two parameters as part of its -init: a key and a BOOL denoting whether the sort is ascending or descending. We can have as many NSSortDescriptor objects as we want as part of the sort, and therefore they are placed within an NSArray prior to the sort being performed.

Adding an NSSortDescriptor is especially useful on Cocoa Touch because the NSFetchedResultsController will continue to keep its results sorted without any intervention on our part. The NSFetchedResultsController is discussed in more depth in Chapter 10, *Core Data and iPhone*, on page 179.

4.4 NSManagedObjectContext

Next to NSManagedObject, NSManagedObjectContext is the one object in the Core Data stack that we access the most. The NSManagedObject-Context is the object we access when we want to save to disk, when we want to read data into memory, and when we want to create new objects. As shown in Figure 4.2, on the facing page, the NSManagedObjectContext is at the top of the Core Data "stack" in that it is accessed directly by our code frequently. It is much less common for us to need to go deeper into the stack.

NSManagedObjectContext isn't thread safe. Each thread that needs access to the data should have its own NSManagedObjectContext. This is generally not an issue since most applications are not multithreaded or their multithreaded portions do not need to interact with NSManagedObjectContext on any thread other than the main thread. However, it is important to keep in mind that, like the UI, NSManagedObjectContext should be accessed only on the thread that created it, which is generally the main thread.

GrokkingRecipes_v1/AppDelegate.m

```objc
- (NSManagedObjectContext*)managedObjectContext
{
  if (managedObjectContext) return managedObjectContext;

  NSPersistentStoreCoordinator *coord = [self persistentStoreCoordinator];

  if (!coord) return nil;

  managedObjectContext = [[NSManagedObjectContext alloc] init];
  [managedObjectContext setPersistentStoreCoordinator: coord];

  NSFetchRequest *request = [[[NSFetchRequest alloc] init] autorelease];
  [request setEntity:[NSEntityDescription entityForName:@"Type"
                                 inManagedObjectContext:managedObjectContext]];

  NSError *error = nil;
  NSArray *result = [managedObjectContext executeFetchRequest:request
                                                        error:&error];
  NSAssert(error == nil, [error localizedDescription]);
  if ([result count]) return managedObjectContext;

  //The types table has not been populated
  NSArray *types;
  types = [[[NSBundle mainBundle] infoDictionary] valueForKey:@"RecipeTypes"];

  for (NSString *type in types) {
    NSManagedObject *object = [NSEntityDescription
                                insertNewObjectForEntityForName:@"Type"
                                inManagedObjectContext:managedObjectContext];
    [object setValue:type forKey:@"name"];
  }

  return managedObjectContext;
}
```

Linking the Type Entity to the Type NSComboBox

Now that we have our Type entity populated on launch, we should bind our user interface to it so that changes to the Type table will be reflected in the user interface. To do this, we need to open the MainMenu.xib file in Interface Builder and select the NSComboBox. Then on the Bindings tab, open the Content Values section, and bind it to the type's NSArrayController with a controller key of arrangedObjects and a model key path of name, as shown in Figure 4.3, on the next page.

Now any changes to the Type table will be reflected in the user interface automatically.

The NSManagedObjectContext itself is fairly straightforward to initialize. However, I also like to load any objects that need to be prepopulated into the repository at this point as well. To review, we start off by grabbing a reference to the NSPersistentStoreCoordinator and initializing the NSManagedObjectContext. Once the NSManagedObjectContext is initialized, we pass in the NSPersistentStoreCoordinator.

If we did not have any data that we needed to load into the NSManagedObjectContext, this would normally be the completion of the method. However, in our application, we want to prepopulate the Type entity before anyone gets a chance to create any recipes. Therefore, once the NSManagedObjectContext has been initialized, we immediately execute an NSFetchRequest against the Type table and see whether there are any results. If there are any, then we complete the method and exit the run loop.

If there are no entities in the Type table, then we know that it needs to be populated. The next step is to grab the list of types from the Info.plist and loop over them. For each entry in the Info.plist, we create a new NSManagedObject and set its name to the value from the Info.plist. Once the loop is complete, the store has been prepopulated, and we can exit this cycle of the run loop.

There are a few other ways to prepopulate the repository. Some are easier and some are more complicated than this method. One example I have used in the past is to simply store a prepared repository in the application bundle. When the user requests a new store, I copy the pre-

Figure 4.3: BINDING THE NSCOMBOBOX TO THE TYPE ENTITY

populated store out of the application bundle to the location specified and then initialize the NSPersistentStoreCoordinator against it. This makes the prepopulation easy, but we need to maintain that internal database and update it any time the data model changes.

Another design to prepopulate data is to keep an XML store within the application bundle instead of the final store type. XML is more pliable than the other store types and can easily be manipulated during development. At runtime, we can stand up a Core Data stack against that internal XML store and then execute a copy of the objects over to the final store. This design involves a bit more code than just copying the file, but it makes the maintenance of the internal store easier.

Each design is viable, and it depends on the final application design and the preferences of the developer as to which serves best.

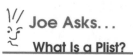

Joe Asks. . .

What Is a Plist?

A *plist* is an XML file that normally represents an NSDictionary data structure. The top level of a plist normally starts out with a <dict> tag and a list of <key> tags along with their values. Since an NSDictionary can hold any object as its value, the value tags can be any number of types including <string>, <array>, and a number of other types including other <dict> tags!

4.5 NSManagedObjectModel

The NSManagedObjectModel can be considered a compiled, binary version of the data model that we created in Xcode. As part of the build process for an application, the .xcdatamodel file is compiled into a .mom file that is stored in the Resources directory of the application bundle. If we have more than one .xcdatamodel file, then each file is compiled into a separate .mom file. When we construct our NSManagedObject-Model, we can use just one of these .mom files, or we can combine them all into a single NSManagedObjectModel. The design of our application usually dictates this decision. For our recipes application, however, we have a single .mom to use as part of our NSManagedObjectModel:

```
GrokkingRecipes_v1/AppDelegate.m
- (NSManagedObjectModel*)managedObjectModel
{
  if (managedObjectModel) return managedObjectModel;

  NSString *path = [[NSBundle mainBundle] pathForResource:@"DataModel"
                                                   ofType:@"mom"];
  NSAssert(path != nil, @"Unable to find DataModel in main bundle");
  if (!path) return nil;

  NSURL *url = [NSURL fileURLWithPath:path];
  managedObjectModel = [[NSManagedObjectModel alloc] initWithContentsOfURL:url];
  return managedObjectModel;
}
```

The construction of the NSManagedObjectModel does not involve very much code when used in one of the standard configurations. We start by determining the location of the .mom file. Since we have only a single data model, we use the NSBundle method -pathForResource:ofType: to locate the path for our model and use it to construct an NSURL. With that NSURL, we can then initialize the NSManagedObjectModel.

Depending on the complexity of the application, it is common to not need access to the NSManagedObjectModel after the Core Data stack has been initialized. However, there is a wealth of information within this object that can be quite useful in edge cases.

For example, since the descriptions of all the entities that exist in the model are contained in the NSManagedObjectModel, it is possible to use it to do dynamic discovery of the model for display purposes. By accessing the NSManagedObjectModel directory, we can interrogate the Core Data stack and discover all the relationships, entities, and properties that exist and display them to the user. Although this might not be useful in a consumer-facing application, it can be quite useful as a developer tool.

Another situation when accessing the NSManagedObjectModel directly is useful is when handling versioning. When we are developing unusual version shifts or writing the versioning code ourselves, it can be very useful to interrogate the NSManagedObjectModel, both the source and the destination, to make logical decisions about the versioning process. Core Data versioning is discussed more in depth in Chapter 5, *Versioning and Migration*, on page 67.

4.6 NSPersistentStoreCoordinator

The NSPersistentStoreCoordinator is at the bottom of the Core Data stack. It is responsible for persisting the data to its repository. That repository is usually, but not always, on disk. The store, in the case of an in-memory store, could be only in memory with no disk representation. However, in most cases, the NSPersistentStoreCoordinator handles disk access.

The NSPersistentStoreCoordinator is also not thread safe. However, the NSManagedObjectContext knows how to properly lock the NSPersistentStoreCoordinator, so therefore it is possible to associate multiple NSManagedObjectContext instances to a single NSPersistentStoreCoordinator without concern. However, direct access to the NSPersistentStoreCoordinator from multiple threads (such as adding persistent store objects) can cause issues. In fact, when working in a multithreaded environment, this is how the single-threaded design of the NSManagedObjectContext is handled. We discuss this aspect of the NSPersistentStoreCoordinator in detail in Chapter 9, *Multithreading and Core Data*, on page 157.

In our Grokking Recipes example application, we build the NSPersistentStoreCoordinator using a known file location and a known persistent store type. This is common in a single persistent store design. However, when we are working in a document model, then each document would have its own persistent store, and each store can be of a different type. Therefore, the creation of the NSPersistentStoreCoordinator can be more complicated in that design. We demonstrate the use of the NSPersistentStoreCoordinator in a document model in Chapter 12, *Recipe: Dynamic Parameters*, on page 225. In our current application, we construct the NSPersistentStoreCoordinator as follows:

GrokkingRecipes_v1/AppDelegate.m
```
- (NSPersistentStoreCoordinator*)persistentStoreCoordinator;
{
  if (persistentStoreCoordinator) return persistentStoreCoordinator;

  NSString *filename = @"GrokkingRecipes.xml";
  NSFileManager *fileManager = [NSFileManager defaultManager];
  NSString *path = [self applicationSupportFolder];
  if ( ![fileManager fileExistsAtPath:path
                          isDirectory:NULL] ) {
    [fileManager createDirectoryAtPath:path
                            attributes:nil];
  }

  path = [path stringByAppendingPathComponent:filename];
  NSURL *url = [NSURL fileURLWithPath:path];
  NSManagedObjectModel *mom = [self managedObjectModel];
  persistentStoreCoordinator = [[NSPersistentStoreCoordinator alloc]
                                initWithManagedObjectModel:mom];

  NSError *error = nil;
  if (![persistentStoreCoordinator addPersistentStoreWithType:NSXMLStoreType
                                                configuration:nil
                                                          URL:url
                                                      options:nil
                                                        error:&error]) {
    [NSApp presentError:error];
  }
  return persistentStoreCoordinator;
}
```

In a single persistent store design, the NSPersistentStoreCoordinator is straightforward in its construction. After confirming that we have not already initialized the store, we check to make sure that the location where the file is to be written exists. The standard location for an application of this design is in the Application Support directory under the Library directory of the user's home.

Once we have confirmed the existence or added the appropriate directories, the next step is to get a reference to the NSManagedObjectModel, which is discussed in Section 4.5, *NSManagedObjectModel*, on page 62. With a reference to the NSManagedObjectModel, we can initialize the NSPersistentStoreCoordinator with that model.

With the NSPersistentStoreCoordinator initialized, we need to add the actual NSPersistentStore to it. It is possible to add more than one NSPersistentStore to the NSPersistentStoreCoordinator, which can be useful when dealing with data that is split into multiple files. However, in our example, we have a single file. Part of adding the NSPersistentStore to the NSPersistentStoreCoordinator is to specify what type of store it is. The different types of stores and their benefits are discussed in Chapter 6, *Performance Tuning*, on page 91. When we add the NSPersistentStore to the NSPersistentStoreCoordinator, it is possible that there will be a failure. Therefore, we check for the error and handle it if it occurs.

Normally once we have initialized the NSPersistentStoreCoordinator and added it to the NSManagedObjectContext, we rarely touch it again. In most cases, the only time we would want to access it again is to handle manual migration.

4.7 Fetched Properties

In addition to NSFetchRequest objects, we have the ability to define a lazy relationship between objects. Fetched properties are kind of a cross between relationships and the NSFetchRequest. A fetched property is not a relationship in the strictest sense and is not realized until the property is requested. When the property is accessed, Core Data performs the underlying NSFetchRequest and returns the result. Unlike a normal relationship, a fetched property is returned as an NSArray as opposed to an NSSet.

In practice, I have found fetched properties to be less useful and less flexible than creating either a stored fetch request or building the fetch request in code. Usually when a situation calls for a fetched property, it tends to be easier to subclass the entity in question, perform an NSFetchRequest in code, and return the results.

4.8 Wrapping Up

We covered a large number of pieces of Core Data in this chapter. As we continue to explore Core Data in depth, please use this chapter as a reference point for pieces of Core Data and how they all fit together. By the end of the book, each of these elements should be as familiar to you as NSString and NSArray are today.

Chapter 5

Versioning and Migration

Just like a battle plan, no code base ever survives contact with users. As soon as users start to use an application, they want to change it. Even if the code is just for ourselves, we, also as users, will want to change things. For example, we may need to add an attribute, add a new object, or just restructure things to accommodate those changes. Those changes can be quite involved and invariably will require a change to how the data is stored. Although the data migration will work even if there is no data stored, it is more useful going forward to have some data to work with. Therefore, if you have not added any recipes yet, I recommend doing so before we proceed.

Starting with Mac OS X 10.5 Leopard, Apple has made data migration nearly trivial for users of Core Data. When developing for Leopard, versioning is included in the Core Data API, and with a relatively small amount of effort on our part as the developer, we can easily migrate our data stores from one version to another. Depending on the complexity of the migration, the effort required of us, the developer, can be trivial to rather complex.

Taking the project that we started with in Chapter 2, *Getting Started with Core Data*, on page 7, we will be adding some additional features to it in succeeding versions. In version 2, we will add the ability to tag an author to a recipe as well as tag a "last used" date. That way, we know who created the delicious dish as well as the last time we made it. We certainly wouldn't want to accidentally make the same dish two days in a row! Lastly, we will remove the Meat and Fish entries from the Type attribute of the Recipe entity. Any recipe entries that are flagged with Meat or Fish will be updated to Entrée instead.

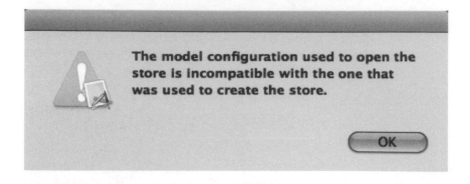

Figure 5.1: DEFAULT MODEL ISSUE DIALOG BOX

In version 3, we will normalize the repository a bit by extracting the ingredients and forming a many-to-many relationship back to the recipes. In addition, we will add the concept of a shopping list to make it easier to ensure we pick up all the ingredients on our next trip to the store. Finally, we will extract the unitOfMeasure attribute from the RecipeIngredient entity into its own entity and allow that new entity to be linked to the new ingredient entity. This will give us one lookup list for the various units of measure and reduce the risk of human error.

5.1 Some Maintenance Before We Migrate

Before we actually release a new version of our application that migrates the data, we need to first complete a minor "maintenance" update for our users. Normally we would add this code to the very first version of our application, but just in case we wrote that first version before versioning was a consideration (or in case we wrote the first version for Tiger), we need to go back to our old version and add a very small amount of code to help our users.

Some users will download the new version of an application to just "try it out" and see whether it is worth the upgrade price or worth the hassle. Normally this is not an issue until we upgrade the data underneath our users. Then things go sideways. What we *do not* want to happen is the error message shown in Figure 5.1.

This is a terrible user experience and something we want to avoid. Fortunately, the way to avoid it is very easy, and we can add it to a point release of our application before we do any migration. That way, when the user opens the first version of our application after "testing" the second version, they get a friendly error message, or you can take it a step further and restore/access the older version of their data.

GrokkingRecipes_v2/AppDelegate.m

```
if (![persistentStoreCoordinator addPersistentStoreWithType:NSXMLStoreType
                                           configuration:nil
                                                    URL:url
                                                options:dict
                                                  error:&error]) {
  NSDictionary *ui = [error userInfo];
  if (ui) {
    NSLog(@"%@:%s %@", [self class], _cmd, [error localizedDescription]);
    for (NSError *suberror in [ui valueForKey:NSDetailedErrorsKey]) {
      NSLog(@"\t%@", [suberror localizedDescription]);
    }
  } else {
    NSLog(@"%@:%s %@", [self class], _cmd, [error localizedDescription]);
  }
  NSAlert *alert = [[NSAlert alloc] init];
  [alert setAlertStyle:NSCriticalAlertStyle];
  [alert setMessageText:@"Unable to load the recipes database."];
  NSString *msgText = nil;
  msgText = [NSString stringWithFormat:@"The recipes database %@%@%@\n%@",
            @"is either corrupt or was created by a newer ",
            @"version of Grokking Recipes.  Please contact ",
            @"support to assist with this error.\n\nError: ",
            [error localizedDescription]];
  [alert setInformativeText:msgText];
  [alert addButtonWithTitle:@"Quit"];
  [alert runModal];
  exit(1);
}
```

We have added this code to the -persistentStoreCoordinator method in the application delegate of our first version of the recipes application. In the first version of our application, if an error occurred with the adding of an NSPersistentStore to the NSPersistentStoreCoordinator, we would just present the error to the user via ((NSApplication sharedApplication) presentError:error). With this change, we give the user a little more useful information as well as dumping quite a bit of useful information to the logs for us to review. We will also keep this code in all future versions of our application to help "future proof" it. Naturally, this is the bare minimum that we can do, and I recommend adding other options. However, the most important point is in place. We do not let the user proceed without a Core Data stack in place. The original way that we

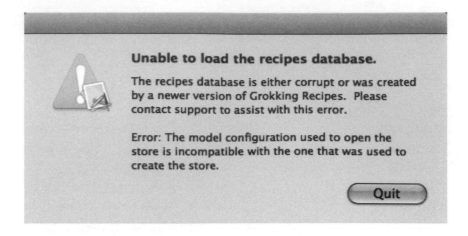

Figure 5.2: NEW, IMPROVED ERROR DIALOG BOX

were handling this error allowed the user to proceed with our application and enter new information only to find out they can't save it. With this error message, we stop that from occurring by forcing the user to quit until they deal with the error. The resulting error message is shown in Figure 5.2.

We do have one other addition to this error check. Before we present the NSAlert to the user, we also dump the information about the error to the console. This is primarily useful during the development cycle but can also be helpful when we have a user with an unusual issue. When Core Data fails with more than one error, it will load all the errors into a single NSError instance that it passes back to us. In that situation, the top-level -localizedDescription will tell the user only that "Multiple Validation Errors Occurred," which is not very useful to us as developers. However, the other errors are available for display, we can get them from the userInfo of the NSError, and we can then iterate over them, print out their -localizedDescription to the console, and reveal the exact problems. We also check to make sure there are suberrors so that we can print out the top-level error by itself if there is only one.

5.2 A Simple Migration

To demonstrate a simple migration, we will add the ability to attribute recipes to authors. To kick off the versioning, the first thing that we

---

Your First Data Model Version

When you first set up versioning, be sure to look inside the target in Xcode and update the Compile Sources section. If you do not see the .xcdatamodeld file inside the target, then remove the xcdatamodel references from it and drag the entire xcdatamodeld bundle into the target. Otherwise, your application may complain about being unable to merge entities because it will treat each version of the model as an independent model.

Once this change has been completed, it is best to clean the project (delete any previously compiled code) by choosing Build > Clean All Targets from the main menu.

---

need to do is create a new managed object model (MOM) based on the first one. To do this, we need to select the existing model in Xcode and then choose Design > Data Model > Add Model Version.

Creating a Versioned Data Model

This is the first time we have added a model version, Xcode is going to create a new bundle for us called DataModel.xcdatamodeld and put the original MOM inside the bundle along with a new copy of the original MOM. To make things clearer in the example project, I renamed these MOM objects to v1.xcdatamodel and v2.xcdatamodel. Next, we need to select the v2.xcdatamodel and choose Design > Data Model > Set Current Version. Like the name suggests, this tells Core Data which version of the MOM is current.

Now that we have a new version of the MOM, it is time to add the new entities and attributes. This is going to require the addition of a new entity and some changes to the Recipe entity. Look at the new model (Figure 5.3, on the following page) and compare it to the original model (Figure 2.4, on page 14). In this updated MOM, you'll find the new Author entity along with its one-to-many relationship with the Recipe entity. Also, the Recipe entity has a new attribute called lastUsed, which is defined as an Date.

We're not quite done yet. If we were to run the application right now, we would trip the error that we discussed in Section 5.1, *Some Maintenance Before We Migrate*, on page 68. Clearly something is missing.

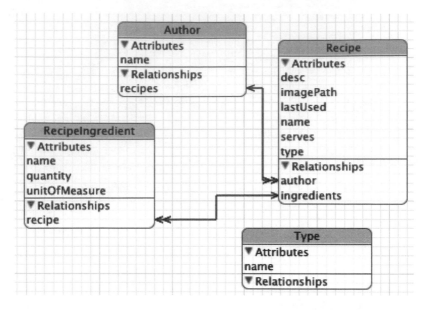

Figure 5.3: VERSION 2 OF THE MOM

Turning on Automatic Data Migration

The first thing we need to do is to tell Core Data to automatically migrate data when the persistent store is not using the same model as the current version. To do this, we need to make a small change to the persistentStoreCoordinator method in our AppDelegate. Previously we were passing nil to the addPersistentStoreWithType:configuration:URL:options:error: method for the options parameter. However, we need to change that to the following:

GrokkingRecipes_v2/AppDelegate.m

```
NSMutableDictionary *dict = [NSMutableDictionary dictionary];
[dict setObject:[NSNumber numberWithBool:YES]
        forKey:NSMigratePersistentStoresAutomaticallyOption];

NSError *error = nil;
if (![persistentStoreCoordinator addPersistentStoreWithType:NSXMLStoreType
                                    configuration:nil
                                              URL:url
                                          options:dict
                                            error:&error]) {
```

This change tells Core Data to attempt an automatic migration when it encounters a persistent store that does not match the current version

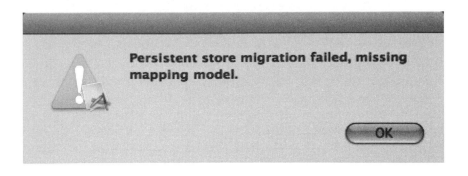

Figure 5.4: ERROR WHEN WE ARE MISSING A MAPPING MODEL

of the MOM. If we try to run our application after this change, we get something new, as shown in Figure 5.4.

Creating Our First Mapping Model

We're definitely getting closer but are not quite there yet. We are missing one more thing, and that is the mapping model. The mapping model describes how to transition the data from one object model to another. A mapping model is created by asking Xcode to create a new file and choosing Mapping Model from the selection. After naming the new file (I named it v1_to_v2), Xcode asks you to select the source and destination models. Selecting v1 and v2 appropriately will complete the file creation. Xcode does some basic building of the mapping model, and that is nearly sufficient for this migration.

The initial mapping model generated by Xcode handles almost everything that we want to do. It handles the migration of the existing entities over to the new object model just fine. However, there are a couple of things we need to do to tweak it.

First, we can remove the Author entity from the mapping model. Since there is no Author in the original object model and the relationship is not required, we do not need to deal with it during the migration. We can also remove the mapping for the author relationship in the Recipe entity as well as the lastUsed attribute. Again, since these can be nil and we are not populating them during the migration, they are not needed in the mapping model.

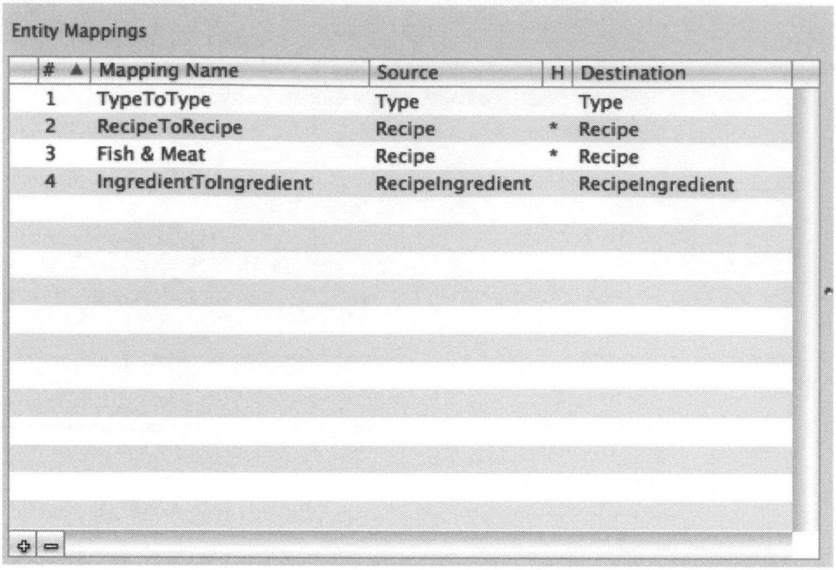

Figure 5.5: MAPPING MODEL ENTITY LIST

Second, we can remove the inverse of the relationship between the Recipe entity and the RecipeIngredient entity. Because this relationship is two sided (as *strongly* recommended by Apple), we do not need to migrate both sides of the relationship. Therefore, we can remove the RecipeIngredient side of the relationship. This will also remove a potential issue with the next change. The resulting entity mapping list is shown in Figure 5.5.

The other change we need to make to the mapping model is a bit more complicated. To remove the Meat and Fish types from the store during the migration, we need to employ a filter predicate. Just like the NSFilterPredicate object that we are used to working with, a filter predicate in the model resolves to a boolean expression that determines whether the source object is included in the mapping. In the recipe mapping, we will add the following predicate:

```
type != 'Fish' && type != 'Meat'
```

This will tell the mapping to migrate all the recipe entities except for those that have a type of Fish or Meat (see Figure 5.6, on the next page). Next, we will create a new mapping that is almost identical to the

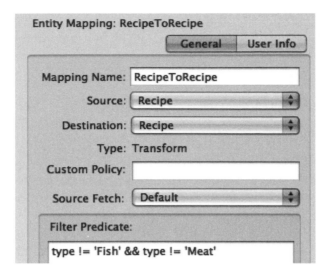

Figure 5.6: EXCLUSION FILTER PREDICATE

RecipeToRecipe mapping. This second mapping of the Recipe entity we will call Fish & Meat, and its predicate will be as follows:

```
type == 'Fish' || type == 'Meat'
```

The other difference between the Fish & Meat mapping and the RecipeTo-Recipe mapping is the type attribute. In the original RecipeToRecipe mapping, it was set to $source.type, which tells Core Data to copy over the value of the source object's type attribute. In the Fish & Meat mapping, we will set it to Entrée directly. This will cause any Recipe entity with a Fish or Meat type to be changed to Entrée during the migration.

Now when we run the application, nothing spectacular happens. The application opens, the data is displayed, and everything is happy without any noise. That is all there is to it for version 2!

What Did We Just Do?

We have just completed a very simple data migration from version 1 to version 2 of our data model. Now, when a user runs our application, no matter what version data model they have, they will automatically be upgraded to version 2 without any surprises.

Along the way, we learned how to create multiple versions of our data model and how to create mapping models to describe how to transition the data between versions.

5.3 Fundamentals of Core Data Versioning

So, what is the magic behind all of this? How does the data migration actually work? As we already explored in the previous chapters, Core Data works with MOM objects that describe the data entities, their attributes, and their relationships. Core Data versioning works with those same MOM objects but takes the design one step further. Each entity version in each data model has a unique hash. When Core Data loads a persistent store from disk, it resolves the matching hashes in the persistent store against the MOM objects included with the application. If the matching MOM is not flagged as the "current" MOM, then data migration kicks in.

How Data Migration Works

Core Data handles data migration in a very straightforward manner. Whenever a persistent store needs to be migrated, there are three steps.

Copying of the Entities with Attributes

In the first pass of the migration, Core Data creates new entities in the new persistent store for every entity in the old store. These entities have their attributes copied over but not their relationships. During this phase, Core Data also keeps a reference to the old unique ID for each entity to be used in phase 2.

Creating Relationships Between the Entities

In the second pass, Core Data builds all the relationships between the entities based on the previous relationships. This is where the reference in phase 1 is used.

Validation of the New Store

During the migration, all validation rules are turned off, and Core Data ignores the child classes defined in the MOM. Therefore, it is possible that some data validation rules got broken during the migration. In the final phase of the migration, Core Data goes back through the store and checks all the validation rules to ensure that the data is in a valid state.

Model Versions and Hashes

The word *versioning* has been used through this chapter as well as other material to describe data migration in Core Data. Unfortunately, it is an inaccurate term. Versioning implies that there is an order or precedence to the models. This is not accurate when it comes to data model versioning/migration in Core Data.

Entity Hashes

Instead of keeping track of a version number, creation date, or some other potentially chronological identifier, Core Data generates a hash for each entity in a model. Those hashes are then stored within the persistent stores created with that model for later comparison. When a persistent store is loaded, the first thing that Core Data does is to retrieve the metadata from that store. Inside that metadata is a list of every entity type in the store along with the hash for that entity. Core Data then compares that list of hashes against the hashes of the "current" MOM. If they match, then everything is fine, and the store is loaded. If they do not match, then Core Data checks the options on the load persistent store call to see whether automatic data migration is requested. If it is not, then the error message from Section 5.1, *Some Maintenance Before We Migrate*, on page 68 is presented to the user.

Changing the Hash Values

Surprisingly, not everything that changes inside a MOM causes the hash of the entities inside to change. There are actually quite a few things that we can do to a model that does not trigger data migration at all.

Changes That Alter the Entity Hash

If any of the following are changed on an entity, the entity will report a different hash:

- Name: The name of the entity
- Inheritance: Changing who the parent entity is
- Persistent properties: Adding or removing a property

In addition, changing the following for properties will also trigger a change to the entity hash:

- Name: The name of the property

- Optionality/read-only: Changing whether the property is optional or read-only

- Attribute type: Changes to the type of value stored

- Relationship: Changes to the destination, minimum/maximum count, the delete rule, or the inverse

Changes That *Do Not* Alter the Entity Hash

The following changes to an entity will *not* trigger a change to the entity hash:

- Class name: Changes to the NSManagedObject subclass

- Transient properties: Properties that are not saved in the persistent store

- User info: Adding, removing, or changing the user info keys/values

- Validation predicates: Adding, removing, or changing the validation rules

- Default values: Adding, removing, or changing the default value of an attribute

In addition, the following changes to the properties of an entity will also *not* change the hash of the entity:

- User info: Adding, removing, or changing the user info key/values

- Validation predicates: Adding, removing, or changing the validation rules

The general distinction between things that do and do not affect version hashes is whether the changes impact the store schema. Things such as the class name impact only the runtime, not the structure of the persistent data.

Mapping Models

If Core Data detects that an upgrade to the persistent store is needed, it looks for three files in the application bundle:

- The MOM that matches the hash from the persistent store

- The current MOM

- The mapping model for those two MOM objects

Assuming that all three files are located (and if they aren't, bad things happen), Core Data will then migrate the data in the persistent store from the old MOM to the new MOM. Once the migration is complete, the stack (MOC, PS, and MOM) is fully initialized, and the application continues. This, of course, is the happy path, and there are several safeguards in place to allow the application developer to control failures.

5.4 A More Complex Migration

Now that we have gotten our feet wet with data migration and versioning, it's time to test the limits of what we can do. To that end, we will create another migration that is far more complex. Specifically, the ingredients really should be in another entity with a many-to-many relationship to the recipe. In addition, the units of measure should also be in their own table. And since we have the engine apart as it were, we can put in the cost of the ingredients as well as the unit size for ordering. This will allow us to estimate the cost per serving.

With these changes in mind, the data model will look like Figure 5.7, on the next page. As we learned earlier in this chapter, we will need a mapping model to go from version 2 to version 3. But what about users who are still on version 1? For automatic versioning to work, we would also need a mapping model from version 1 to version 3. Since that will be a variation on our version 2 to version 3 model, we will skip it for the moment.

The biggest challenge for this migration is the introduction of the new entities. Unlike the Author entity from before, during this migration, not only are we creating new entities, but we are having to extract data from existing entities to build those new entities, and we have to then properly link the new entities back to their source. To make it even more interesting, we do not want these new entities duplicated. This complexity is far beyond the basic migration that we did for version 2, and it is going to require writing a custom NSEntityMigrationPolicy to handle it.

NSEntityMigrationPolicy

A NSEntityMigrationPolicy allows us to control exactly how a migration is handled. Although there are quite a few methods that we can override

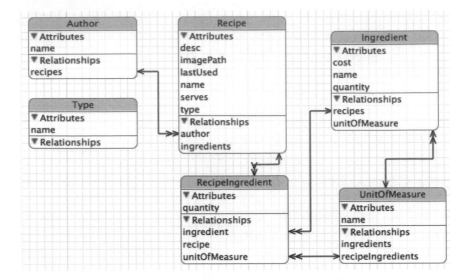

Figure 5.7: VERSION 3 OF THE MOM

depending on our needs, the two methods that we need for this migration are as follows:

```
- (BOOL)createDestinationInstancesForSourceInstance:(NSManagedObject*)source
                        entityMapping:(NSEntityMapping*)mapping
                          manager:(NSMigrationManager*)manager
                          error:(NSError**)error

- (BOOL)createRelationshipsForDestinationInstance:(NSManagedObject*)dInstance
                        entityMapping:(NSEntityMapping*)mapping
                          manager:(NSMigrationManager*)manager
                          error:(NSError**)error
```

createDestinationInstancesForSourceInstance:

The first method, createDestinationInstancesForSourceInstance:, is called for each entity in the source store that is associated with this migration policy. For example, during the migration of the RecipeIngredient entities and the creation of the Ingredient entities, this method would be called for each RecipeIngredient, and it would be expected that an ingredient entity would be created or associated with the incoming RecipeIngredient as a result.

The code to implement this breaks down as follows:

GrokkingRecipes_v3/RecipeIngredientToIngredient.m

```
NSManagedObjectContext *destMOC = [manager destinationContext];
NSString *destEntityName = [mapping destinationEntityName];

//The name of the ingredient
NSString *name = [source valueForKey:@"name"];
```

In the first part of the method, we are simply setting up references that will be needed later. Specifically, we are getting a reference to the destination NSManagedObjectContext, which we will need to create new entities, the name of the destination entity, and most important the name value from the incoming entity. Since the incoming entity is a RecipeIngredient, the name value will be the name of the ingredient that we now want to reference.

GrokkingRecipes_v3/RecipeIngredientToIngredient.m

```
NSMutableDictionary *userInfo = (NSMutableDictionary*)[manager userInfo];
if (!userInfo) {
  userInfo = [NSMutableDictionary dictionary];
  [manager setUserInfo:userInfo];
}
NSMutableDictionary *ingredientLookup = [userInfo valueForKey:@"ingredients"];
if (!ingredientLookup) {
  ingredientLookup = [NSMutableDictionary dictionary];
  [userInfo setValue:ingredientLookup forKey:@"ingredients"];
}
NSManagedObject *dest = [ingredientLookup valueForKey:name];
if (!dest) {
  dest = [NSEntityDescription insertNewObjectForEntityForName:destEntityName
                                     inManagedObjectContext:destMOC];
  [dest setValue:name forKey:@"name"];
  [ingredientLookup setValue:dest forKey:name];
}
```

In this next section of code, we deal with the possibility that the Ingredient entity that we need to reference has already been created. Rather than doing a fetch against the destination context every time, we have a hash built up and stored within the NSMigrationManger. The NSMigrationManager has an NSDictionary called userInfo that is perfectly suited for this purpose. We first lazily initialize this dictionary, and then we lazily initialize another NSDictionary inside it to store references to the Ingredient entities using the name of the ingredient as the key. With this, we can make sure that each Ingredient is created only once. If the Ingredient does not exist yet, then we create it and store it back inside of the userInfo cache.

GrokkingRecipes_v3/RecipeIngredientToIngredient.m

```
[manager associateSourceInstance:source
        withDestinationInstance:dest
              forEntityMapping:mapping];

return YES;
```

The last thing that we need to do is to tell the manager about the association. Since the manager keeps track of all associations between the two NSManagedObjectContext objects, we need to inform it of this new entity that was just created and that it is associated with the source entity that was passed in. Once that is complete, we return YES, and we are done.

createRelationshipsForDestinationInstance:

In a properly designed data model, this method will rarely if ever be needed. The intention of this method (which is called in the second pass) is to build any relationships for the new destination entity that was created in the previous method. However, if all the relationships in the model are double sided, then this is not necessary because we already set up one side of them. If for some reason there is an entity in the model that is not double sided, then additional code would be required in this method to handle the one-sided relationship. Since we do not need that functionality in our model, we just return YES.

GrokkingRecipes_v3/RecipeIngredientToIngredient.m

```
- (BOOL)createRelationshipsForDestinationInstance:(NSManagedObject*)dInstance
                                    entityMapping:(NSEntityMapping*)mapping
                                          manager:(NSMigrationManager*)manager
                                            error:(NSError**)error
{
    return YES;
}
```

5.5 Automatic Data Migration

If your data migration needs are easy to handle and your application is not coming from Tiger, then automatic migration is probably all that is needed. Automatic migration lets Core Data handle all the details and assumes the following:

- Every persistent store that the application will come up against has hash metadata.

- Every persistent store that the application will come up against has a corresponding model stored inside the application's bundle.

- Every persistent store that the application will come up against has a mapping model from its MOM to the current MOM.

If the application can meet these three criteria (and any application that has begun its life in Leopard should), then automatic migration should be able to do all of the dirty work for us.

To enable automatic versioning, we need to set a preference on the NSPersistentStoreCoordinator while adding a persistent store. Previously, the method that built up the NSPersistentStoreCoordinator in our recipe application was as follows:

`GrokkingRecipes_v1/AppDelegate.m`

```
- (NSPersistentStoreCoordinator*)persistentStoreCoordinator;
{
  if (persistentStoreCoordinator) return persistentStoreCoordinator;

  NSString *filename = @"GrokkingRecipes.xml";
  NSFileManager *fileManager = [NSFileManager defaultManager];
  NSString *path = [self applicationSupportFolder];
  if ( ![fileManager fileExistsAtPath:path
                          isDirectory:NULL] ) {
    [fileManager createDirectoryAtPath:path
                            attributes:nil];
  }

  path = [path stringByAppendingPathComponent:filename];
  NSURL *url = [NSURL fileURLWithPath:path];
  NSManagedObjectModel *mom = [self managedObjectModel];
  persistentStoreCoordinator = [[NSPersistentStoreCoordinator alloc]
                                  initWithManagedObjectModel:mom];

  NSError *error = nil;
  if (![persistentStoreCoordinator addPersistentStoreWithType:NSXMLStoreType
                                                configuration:nil
                                                          URL:url
                                                      options:nil
                                                        error:&error]) {
    [NSApp presentError:error];
  }
  return persistentStoreCoordinator;
}
```

With automatic versioning, we need to make one minor change to this method. Instead of passing nil as the options value in the call to -addPersistentStoreWithType:configuration:URL:options:error:, we build up an NSDictionary with one key and value. By setting the key NSMigratePersistentStoresAutomaticallyOption to YES, Core Data will attempt to migrate the persistent store if needed.

GrokkingRecipes_v2/AppDelegate.m

```
NSMutableDictionary *dict = [NSMutableDictionary dictionary];
[dict setObject:[NSNumber numberWithBool:YES]
        forKey:NSMigratePersistentStoresAutomaticallyOption];

NSError *error = nil;
if (![persistentStoreCoordinator addPersistentStoreWithType:NSXMLStoreType
                                              configuration:nil
                                                        URL:url
                                                    options:dict
                                                      error:&error]) {
```

5.6 Manual Data Migration

If the persistent store that is being migrated was originally written in Tiger, then it will not contain the hash information that Core Data needs, and automatic migration will fail. Fortunately, these stores can still be migrated, but it is a manual process.

Another situation where manual migration will be useful is when dealing with very large stores. During the migration process, the entire store is pulled into memory. With very large stores, this can cause a performance issue as well as a usability issue. Therefore, in those situations, it may be advantageous to migrate the store in chunks so that the memory is more manageable. Doing that would require a manual migration process and a custom NSMigrationManager.

5.7 Progressive Data Migration

What happens when your application is at version 5 of its data model and someone who has been at version 1 decides to upgrade? Normally you would need to provide a mapping model for every combination of source and destination object models. For the first couple of versions, this is not an issue. However, when you are getting further and further away from version 1, this becomes increasingly difficult. Fortunately, it is possible to figure out a migration path and do a progressive migration.

To accomplish this, we will need to handle the migration manually. The workflow is as follows:

1. If the store's model is the current model, do nothing.

2. Find a mapping model with the current store's model as its source.

3. Migrate the data to that mapping model's destination model.

4. Repeat starting at step 1.

Creating the Migration Method

To begin this monumental task, we will be creating a new method in the AppDelegate. The method requires several pieces of information: the source path, the source type (XML, SQL, and so on), and the final model. In addition, we will pass in an error to be able to report any failures.

ProgressiveMigration/AppDelegate.m

```
- (BOOL)progressivelyMigrateURL:(NSURL*)sourceStoreURL
                    ofType:(NSString*)type
                    toModel:(NSManagedObjectModel*)finalModel
                    error:(NSError**)error
{
```

It's a rather unwieldy method name to be sure, but it contains all the information that we need to figure out our migration path. Since this is going to be a recursive method, the first thing we need to do is check to see whether we are at our goal:

ProgressiveMigration/AppDelegate.m

```
NSDictionary *sourceMetadata =
[NSPersistentStoreCoordinator metadataForPersistentStoreOfType:type
                                                    URL:sourceStoreURL
                                                    error:error];

if (!sourceMetadata) return NO;

if ([finalModel isConfiguration:nil
    compatibleWithStoreMetadata:sourceMetadata]) {
  *error = nil;
  return YES;
}
```

In this code segment, we first retrieve the metadata from the source URL. If that metadata is not nil, we ask the final model whether the metadata is compatible with it. If it is, then we are happy and done. We then set the error pointer to nil and return YES. If not, then we need to try to figure out the mapping model and potentially the interim data model to migrate to.

Finding All the Managed Object Models

To find the next step in the migration, we need to find every managed object model in the bundle and loop through them. The goal at this point is to get all the models and then figure out which one we can migrate to. Since these models will probably be in their own bundles, we have to first look for the bundles and then look inside each of them.

ProgressiveMigration/AppDelegate.m

```
//Find the source model
NSManagedObjectModel *sourceModel = [NSManagedObjectModel
                                    mergedModelFromBundles:nil
                                    forStoreMetadata:sourceMetadata];
NSAssert(sourceModel != nil, ([NSString stringWithFormat:
                             @"Failed to find source model\n%@",
                             sourceMetadata]));

//Find all of the mom and momd files in the Resources directory
NSMutableArray *modelPaths = [NSMutableArray array];
NSArray *momdArray = [[NSBundle mainBundle] pathsForResourcesOfType:@"momd"
                                                   inDirectory:nil];
for (NSString *momdPath in momdArray) {
  NSString *resourceSubpath = [momdPath lastPathComponent];
  NSArray *array = [[NSBundle mainBundle]
                   pathsForResourcesOfType:@"mom"
                   inDirectory:resourceSubpath];
  [modelPaths addObjectsFromArray:array];
}
NSArray* otherModels = [[NSBundle mainBundle] pathsForResourcesOfType:@"mom"
                                                    inDirectory:nil];
[modelPaths addObjectsFromArray:otherModels];

if (!modelPaths || ![modelPaths count]) {
  //Throw an error if there are no models
  NSMutableDictionary *dict = [NSMutableDictionary dictionary];
  [dict setValue:@"No models found in bundle"
          forKey:NSLocalizedDescriptionKey];
  //Populate the error
  *error = [NSError errorWithDomain:@"Zarra" code:8001 userInfo:dict];
  return NO;
}
```

In this code block, we first grab all the resource paths from the mainBundle that are of type momd. This will give us a list of all the model bundles. We then loop through this list and look for mom resources inside each and add those to an overall array. Once those are done, we then look inside the mainBundle again for any freestanding mom resources. Finally, we do a failure check to make sure we have some models to look through. If we can't find any, then we populate the NSError and return NO.

Finding the Mapping Model

Now the complicated part comes in. Since it is not currently possible to get an NSMappingModel with just the source model and then determine the destination model, we have to instead loop through every model we find, instantiate it, plug it in as a possible destination, and see whether there is a mapping model in existence. If there isn't, we continue to the next one.

ProgressiveMigration/AppDelegate.m

```
NSMappingModel *mappingModel = nil;
NSManagedObjectModel *targetModel = nil;
NSString *modelPath = nil;
for (modelPath in modelPaths) {
  targetModel = [[NSManagedObjectModel alloc]
                initWithContentsOfURL:[NSURL fileURLWithPath:modelPath]];
  mappingModel = [NSMappingModel mappingModelFromBundles:nil
                                    forSourceModel:sourceModel
                                    destinationModel:targetModel];
  //If we found a mapping model then proceed
  if (mappingModel) break;
  //Release the target model and keep looking
  [targetModel release], targetModel = nil;
}
//We have tested every model, if nil here we failed
if (!mappingModel) {
  NSMutableDictionary *dict = [NSMutableDictionary dictionary];
  [dict setValue:@"No models found in bundle"
          forKey:NSLocalizedDescriptionKey];
  *error = [NSError errorWithDomain:@"Zarra"
                              code:8001
                          userInfo:dict];
  return NO;
}
```

This section is probably the most complicated piece of the progressive migration routine. In this section, we're looping through all the models that were previously discovered. For each of those models, we're instantiating the model and then asking NSMappingModel for an instance that will map between our known source model and the current model. If we find a mapping model, we break from our loop and continue. Otherwise, we release the instantiated model and continue the loop. After the loop, if the mapping model is still nil, we generate an error stating that we cannot discover the progression between the source model and the target and return NO. At this point, we should have all the components we need for one migration. The source model, target model, and mapping model are all known quantities. Now it's time to migrate!

Performing the Migration

In this block, we are instantiating an NSMigrationManager (if we needed something special, we would build our own manager instead) with the source model and the destination model. We are also building up a unique path to migrate to. In this example, we are using the destination model's filename as the unique change to the source store's path. Once the destination path is built, we then tell the migration manager to perform the migration and check to see whether it was successful. If it wasn't, we simply return NO because the NSError will be populated by the NSMigrationManager. If it's successful, there are only three things left to do: move the source out of the way, then replace it with the new destination store, and finally recurse.

`ProgressiveMigration/AppDelegate.m`

```
NSMigrationManager *manager = [[NSMigrationManager alloc]
                              initWithSourceModel:sourceModel
                              destinationModel:targetModel];

NSString *modelName = [[modelPath lastPathComponent]
                       stringByDeletingPathExtension];
NSString *storeExtension = [[sourceStoreURL path] pathExtension];
NSString *storePath = [[sourceStoreURL path] stringByDeletingPathExtension];
//Build a path to write the new store
storePath = [NSString stringWithFormat:@"%@.%@.%@", storePath,
             modelName, storeExtension];
NSURL *destinationStoreURL = [NSURL fileURLWithPath:storePath];

if (![manager migrateStoreFromURL:sourceStoreURL
                             type:type
                          options:nil
                  withMappingModel:mappingModel
                 toDestinationURL:destinationStoreURL
                  destinationType:type
               destinationOptions:nil
                            error:error]) {
    return NO;
}
```

In this final code block, we first create a permanent location for the original store to be moved to. In this case, we will use a globally unique string generated from the NSProcessInfo class and attach the destination model's filename and the store's extension to it. Once that path is built, we move the source to it and then replace the source with the destination. At this point, we are at the same spot we were when we began except that we are now one version closer to the current model version.

Now we need to loop back to step 1 again in our workflow. Therefore, we will recursively call ourselves, returning the result of that recurse. As you can recall from the beginning of this method, if we are now at the current version, we will simply return YES, which will end the recursion.

`ProgressiveMigration/AppDelegate.m`

```
NSString *guid = [[NSProcessInfo processInfo] globallyUniqueString];
guid = [guid stringByAppendingPathExtension:modelName];
guid = [guid stringByAppendingPathExtension:storeExtension];
NSString *appSupportPath = [storePath stringByDeletingLastPathComponent];
NSString *backupPath = [appSupportPath stringByAppendingPathComponent:guid];

NSFileManager *fileManager = [NSFileManager defaultManager];
if (![fileManager moveItemAtPath:[sourceStoreURL path]
                          toPath:backupPath
                           error:error]) {
  //Failed to copy the file
  return NO;
}
//Move the destination to the source path
if (![fileManager moveItemAtPath:storePath
                          toPath:[sourceStoreURL path]
                           error:error]) {
  //Try to back out the source move first, no point in checking it for errors
  [fileManager moveItemAtPath:backupPath
                       toPath:[sourceStoreURL path]
                        error:nil];
  return NO;
}
//We may not be at the "current" model yet, so recurse
return [self progressivelyMigrateURL:sourceStoreURL
                              ofType:type
                             toModel:finalModel
                               error:error];
```

This progressive migration can be tested by first running version 1 of our Grokking Recipes application, entering some data, and then running the ProgressiveMigration version. You will then see the data model migrate seamlessly from version 1 to version 3 with no intervention required.

5.8 Tips and Tricks

Updating a Mapping Model

As always happens during development, you will want to make changes to the current object model that of course will then break the mapping model. Fortunately, it is possible to tell the mapping model to refresh the source and/or destination data models. This can be done via the Design > Mapping Model menu.

Chapter 6

Performance Tuning

Brent Simmons, creator of NetNewsWire, once shared a story about a user who filed a bug report about the poor startup performance of NetNewsWire. Upon discussion with that user, he discovered that they had more than 900,000 unread RSS feeds! The lesson I took away from that story is to expect my users to put thousands of times as much data into my applications as I would ever consider reasonable.

While we are working with Core Data, we need to consider the performance impacts of our design. We might test with a couple of dozen recipes and expect our users to load a couple hundred recipes into our application and test with those expectations. However, our users cannot read our intentions or expectations. As soon as we ship the application, some user somewhere will load 100,000 recipes into it and then file a bug report that it performs poorly.

6.1 Persistent Store Types

Four types of repositories are included with the Core Data API: SQLite, XML, binary, and in-memory. In-memory is technically not a persistent store because it is never written out to disk. Binary is effectively a serialized version of the object graph written out to disk. The XML store writes out the object graph to a human-readable text file, and SQLite stores the object graph in a relational database. Excluding edge cases, it is common to use XML as our persistent store while we are in development and then to switch over to SQLite once the application is ready for production use.

Atomic Stores

Atomic stores include XML, binary, and custom data stores. All of these stores are written to disk atomically; in other words, the entire data file is rewritten on every save. Although these store types have their advantages, they do not scale as well as the SQLite store. In addition, they are loaded fully into memory when they are accessed. This causes atomic stores to have a larger memory footprint than a SQLite store.

However, because they reside completely in memory while the application is running, they can be very fast since the disk is hit only when the file is read into memory and when it is saved back out. SQLite, although still considered a fast store, is slower when dealing with smaller data sets because of its inherent disk access. That said, the differences are measured in fractions of a second, so we cannot expect a large speed increase by using an atomic store. But if fractions of a second matter, it may be something to consider.

When deciding between a binary store and an XML store, the format on disk should be considered. When working with a binary format, the only way to review the data is via Core Data. XML, on the other hand, can be reviewed with any text editor, which makes it a superior choice during development.

SQLite Persistent Store

The single biggest performance boost that we can make to our application is to switch its persistent store type from XML to SQLite. SQLite is a software library that implements a self-contained, serverless, zero-configuration, transactional SQL database engine. SQLite is the most widely deployed SQL database engine in the world. The source code for SQLite is in the public domain.

Better Scaling

By utilizing a relational database as the persistent store, we no longer need to load the entire data set into memory to work with it. Because the data is being stored in a relational database, our application can scale to a very large size. SQLite itself has been tested with data sets measured in terabytes and can handle just about anything that we can realistically develop. Since we are loading only the data we want at a particular moment, SQLite keeps the memory footprint of our application quite low. Likewise, SQLite makes efficient use of its disk space and therefore has a small footprint on disk as well.

More Performance-Tuning Options

By working with a database instead of a flat file, we have access to many more performance-tuning options. For example, we can index the columns within our entities to enable faster predicates. We can also control exactly what gets loaded into memory. It is possible to get just a count of the objects, just the unique identifiers for objects, and more. This flexibility allows us to tune the performance of our application more than any other store type. Because the SQLite store is the only format that is not fully loaded into memory, we get to control the data flow. All of the other formats require that the entire data file be loaded into memory before they can be used. The details of how to utilize these features are discussed in Section 6.3, *Fetching*, on page 98.

6.2 Optimizing Your Data Model

When we are designing our data model, we need to consider several factors. Where we put our binary data can be extremely important because its size and storage location will play a key role in the performance of our application. Likewise, relationships must be carefully balanced and used appropriately. Also, entity inheritance, a powerful feature of Core Data, must be used with a delicate hand because the underlying structure may be surprising.

Although it is easy to think of Core Data as a database API, we must remember that it is not and that structuring the data with data normalization may not yield the most efficient results. In many cases, denormalizing the data can yield greater performance gains.

Where to Put Binary Data

One of the easiest ways to kill performance in a Core Data application is to stick large amounts of binary data into frequently accessed tables. For example, if we were to put the pictures of our recipes into the recipe table, we would start seeing performance degradation after only a couple hundred recipes had been added. Every time we accessed a Recipe entity, we would have to load its image data, even if we were not going to display the image. Since our application displays all the recipes in a list, this would mean that every image would reside in memory immediately upon launch and would remain there until the application quit. Imagine this situation with a few thousand recipes!

> ### ⚞ Joe Asks. . .
> #### What Is a Fault?
>
> Core Data faults are similar to virtual memory page faults. Faulted objects are scoped objects that may or may not actually be in memory, or "realized," until you actually use them. Although there is no guarantee for when a faulted NSManagedObject will be loaded into memory, it is guaranteed to be loaded when accessed. However, the object will be an instance of the appropriate class (either an NSManagedObject or the designated subclass), but its attributes are not initialized.

But where do we draw the line? What is considered a small enough piece of binary data to fit into a table, and what should not be put into the repository at all?

Small Binary Data

Anything smaller than 100 kilobytes is considered to be small binary data. Icons or small avatars are a couple examples of data of this size. When working with something this small, it is most efficient to store it directly as a property value in its corresponding table. The performance impact of binary data this size is negligible. The transformable attribute type is ideal for this use.

Medium Binary Data

Medium binary data is anything that is larger than 100 kilobytes and smaller than 1 megabyte in size. Average-sized images and small audio clips are a few examples of data in this size range. Data of this size can also be stored directly in the repository. However, the data should be stored in its own table on the other end of a relationship with the primary tables. This allows the binary data to remain a fault until it is actually needed. In the previous recipe example, even though the Recipe entity would be loaded into memory for display, the image would be loaded only when it is needed by the UI.

SQLite has shown itself to be quite efficient at disk access. There are cases where loading data from the SQLite store can actually be faster than direct disk access. This is one of the reasons that medium binary data can be stored directly in the repository.

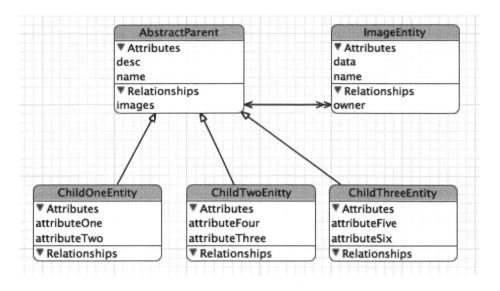

Figure 6.1: ENTITY INHERITANCE EXAMPLE

Large Binary Data

Large binary data is anything greater than 1 megabyte in size. Large images, audio files, and video files are just some examples of data of this size. Any binary data of this size should be stored on disk as opposed to in the repository. When working with data of this size, it is best to store its path information directly in the primary entity (such as the Recipe entity) and store the binary data in a known location on disk (such as in the Application Support subdirectory for your application).

Entity Inheritance

Entity inheritance is a very powerful feature within Core Data. It allows you to build an object-like inheritance tree in your data model. However, this feature comes at a rather large cost. For example, let's look at an example model that makes moderate use of entity inheritance, as shown in Figure 6.1.

The object model itself looks quite reasonable. We are sharing name, desc, and a one-to-many relationship to the ImageEntity. However, the underlying table structure actually looks like Figure 6.2, on the following page. The reason for this is how Core Data handles the object model to relational table mapping. Instead of creating one table for each child

	name	desc	attributeOne	attributeTwo	attributeThree	attributeFour	attributeFive	attributeSix
Entity One								
Entity Two								
Entity Three								

Figure 6.2: SQLite TABLE LAYOUT

object, Core Data creates one large table that includes all the properties for the parent entity as well as its children. The end result is an extremely wide and tall table in the database with a high percentage of empty values.

Although the entity inheritance feature of Core Data is extremely useful, we should be aware of what is going on underneath the object model to avoid a performance penalty. We should not treat entity inheritance as an equal to object inheritance. There is certainly some overlap, but they are not equal, and treating them as such will have a negative impact on the performance of the repository.

Denormalizing Data to Improve Performance

Although the most powerful persistent store available for Core Data is a database, we must always be conscious of the fact that Core Data is not just a database. Core Data is an object hierarchy that can be persisted to a database format. The difference is subtle but important. Core Data is first a collection of objects that we use to display data in a user interface of some form and allow the user to access that data. Therefore, although database normalization might be the first place to look for performance improvements, we should not take it too far. There are six levels of database normalization,[1] but a Core Data repository should rarely, if ever, be taken beyond the second level. There are several cases where we can gain a greater performance benefit by denormalizing the data.

Search Only Properties

Searching within properties can be quite expensive. For properties that have a large amount of text or, worse, Unicode text, a single search field can cause a huge performance hit. One way to improve this situation is to create a derived attribute based on the text in an entity.

---

1. See http://en.wikipedia.org/wiki/Database_normalization for details.

For example, searching in our description property of the Recipe entity can potentially be very expensive if the user has verbose descriptions and/or uses Unicode characters in the description.

To improve performance of searches in this field, we could create a second property on the Recipe entity that strips the Unicode characters from the description and also removes common words such as *a*, *the*, and *etc.* If we then perform the search on this derived property, we can drastically improve search performance.

The downside to using search-only properties is that we need to maintain them. Every time the description field is edited, we need to update the derived property as well.

Expensive Calculations

In a normalized database, calculated values are not stored. It is considered cheaper to recalculate the value as needed than to store it in the database. However, from a user experience point of view, the opposite can frequently be true. In cases where the calculation takes a human noticeable amount of time, it may very well be better for the user to store that calculation in the entity and recalculate it only when one of its dependent values has changed. For example, if we store the first and last names of a user in our Core Data repository, then it might make sense to store the full name as well.

Intelligent Relationships

Relationships in a Core Data Model are like salt in a cooking recipe. Too much and you ruin the recipe; too little and something is missing. Fortunately, there are some simple rules we can follow when it comes to relationships in a Core Data repository.

Follow the Object Model

Core Data is first and foremost an object model. The entities in our model should represent the data as accurately as possible. Just because a value might be duplicated across several objects (or rows from the database point of view) does not mean it should be extruded into its own table. Many times it is more efficient for us to store that string several times over in the entity itself than to traverse a relationship to get it.

Traversing a relationship is generally more expensive than accessing an attribute on the entity. Therefore, if the value being stored is simple, then leave it in the entity it is associated with.

Separate Commonly Used from Rarely Used Data

If the object design calls for a one-to-many relationship or a many-to-many relationship, then definitely create a relationship for it. This is usually the case where the data is more than a single property or contains binary data or would be difficult to properly model inside the parent object. For example, if we have a user entity, it is more efficient to store their address in its own object as opposed to having several attributes in the user object for address, city, state, postal code, and so on.

Balance needs to be carefully maintained between what is stored on the other end of a relationship and what is stored in the primary entity. Crossing key paths is more expensive than accessing attributes, but creating objects that are very wide also slows down data access.

6.3 Fetching

Fetching is the term used to describe the resolving of NSManagedObject objects from the repository. When we retrieve an NSManagedObject, it is "fetched" into memory, and we can then access its properties. To help us utilize memory efficiently, fetching may not always happen all at once. Specifically, when we are using a SQLite store, it is quite possible that an object we think is in memory is actually only on disk and has yet to be read into memory. Likewise, objects that we think we are done with may actually still sit in a cache.

To demonstrate the differences in the ways that we can load data into memory from our SQLite Store, I used Apple's demonstration application from WWDC 2007 called GoFetch.[2] The entire goal of this application is to generate a large amount of random data and let us control how it is fetched back into memory. Each fetch is then timed to demonstrate the speed of various options. These tests were performed with 3,417 records in the SQLite repository.

---

2. The source code for this application is available as part of the ADC Headstart package for Core Data.

Loading NSManagedObjectID Objects Only

The smallest amount of data that we can retrieve as part of an NSFetch-Request is just the NSManagedObjectID. The NSManagedObjectID is the unique identifier for the record and contains no content. In the test discussed earlier, it took the test machine 0.004 seconds to retrieve 3,417 records from disk.

How to Retrieve NSManagedObjectID Objects

There is only one change required to retrieve just NSManagedObjectID objects instead of full NSManagedObject objects:

```
NSFetchRequest *fetchRequest = [[NSFetchRequest alloc] init];
[fetchRequest setEntity:[NSEntityDescription entityForName:@"Person"
 inManagedObjectContext:[self managedObjectContext]]];
[fetchRequest setResultType:NSManagedObjectIDResultType];
```

By changing the -resultType to NSManagedObjectIDResultType, our call to -executeFetchRequest:error: will return an NSArray of NSManagedObjectID objects instead of NSManagedObject objects.

Why would we want only the NSManagedObjectID objects? There are several uses for this:

- Inclusion comparison. Since NSManagedObjectID objects guarantee uniqueness, we can use them to determine whether an object is included in a set and avoid having to retrieve the entire set for this comparison.

- Prefetching. Even though the properties for the associated objects are not loaded into NSManagedObject objects for us to access, they are loaded into a cache within Core Data. This means that when we do access the associated NSManagedObject objects via a call to objectWithID: on NSManagedObjectContext, we will get the results much faster than if we had to make a full round-trip to the disk.

  You can accomplish this by turning on property loading while keeping the -resultType as NSManagedObjectIDResultType. This is often referred to as *warming up the cache*.

Loaded As a Fault

The next smallest amount of data that we can retrieve is referred to as a *faulted* NSManagedObject. What this means is that the NSFetchRequest returns an NSArray of NSManagedObject objects, but those objects contain only the NSManagedObjectID. All the properties and relationships are empty or in a faulted state. As soon as an attribute is accessed, *all of the attributes on that object are loaded in.* Likewise, as soon as a relationship is accessed, all the NSManagedObject objects on the other end of that relationship are loaded in as faults. Performing the same query as earlier in this configuration returned the 3,417 records in 0.007 seconds. Faults will be discussed in greater depth in Section 6.4, *Faulting*, on page 102.

How to Retrieve Faulted NSManagedObject Objects

To disable the fetching of attributes as part of the NSFetchRequest, we need to disable it prior to executing the fetch:

```
NSFetchRequest *fetchRequest = [[NSFetchRequest alloc] init];
[fetchRequest setIncludesPropertyValues:NO];
[fetchRequest setEntity:[NSEntityDescription entityForName:@"Person"
 inManagedObjectContext:[self managedObjectContext]]];
```

Although this seems like a great solution, it can be a bit of a trap. Because this configuration returns empty skeletons, each object gets loaded from disk individually. This is *significantly* slower than loading all the objects needed at once. However, the time to load the objects is spread out and can be less noticeable to the user. For raw speed, it is recommended that we load all the data for the objects in one pass.

Loading Property Values

The next step up from faulted NSManagedObject objects is to prefetch their property values. This will not retrieve the objects on the other sides of relationships. Performing this query took 0.021 seconds for the 3,417 records in the test repository.

How to Retrieve Only Property Values

Retrieving NSManagedObject objects with attributes populated is the default for NSFetchRequest:

```
NSFetchRequest *fetchRequest = [[NSFetchRequest alloc] init];
[fetchRequest setEntity:[NSEntityDescription entityForName:@"Person"
 inManagedObjectContext:[self managedObjectContext]]];
```

This option is a very good middle ground between fetching faults and some of the following choices. In situations where only the object requested needs to be displayed right away and its relationships are not needed right away, this can be the most efficient solution.

How to Load Property Values and NSManagedObjectID Objects

We can also combine this option with the NSManagedObjectID retrieval listed earlier to warm up the cache. The settings to accomplish this are as follows:

```
NSFetchRequest *fetchRequest = [[NSFetchRequest alloc] init];
[fetchRequest setResultType:NSManagedObjectIDResultType];
[fetchRequest setEntity:[NSEntityDescription entityForName:@"Person"
 inManagedObjectContext:[self managedObjectContext]]];
```

This can be used to excellent effect on a background thread when the entire fetch is going to take a significant amount of time. Once the NSManagedObjectID objects are retrieved, they can be safely passed to the primary thread and used to display the data to the user. Using Core Data within a multithreaded application is discussed in greater detail in Chapter 9, *Multithreading and Core Data*, on page 157.

Loading Relationships

The next step up in the scale of loading data is to prefetch the relationships while loading the targeted entities. This does not fetch them as fully formed but as faults. This step up can have a significant impact on the performance of a Core Data application. In the test, this fetch took 1.166 seconds to retrieve 3,417 objects each with only a *single* object on the other side of a one-to-one relationship. With a more complex data model, this becomes an even larger performance hit.

How to Load Relationships

Fortunately, this option gives us some fine-grained control over which relationships to load. This would allow us to, for example, load only the addresses associated with a person and skip over their images, phone numbers, and so on. Accomplishing this requires passing an NSArray of NSString objects with the names of the relationships to load:

```
NSFetchRequest *fetchRequest = [[NSFetchRequest alloc] init];
NSArray *relationshipKeys = [NSArray arrayWithObject:@"addresses"];
[fetchRequest setRelationshipKeyPathsForPrefetching:relationshipKeys];
[fetchRequest setEntity:[NSEntityDescription entityForName:@"Person"
 inManagedObjectContext:[self managedObjectContext]]];
```

In this example code, we create a new NSArray that has one NSString within it that corresponds to the name of the relationship within the Person entity. We can get even more clever with this request by using a keypath in the NSArray and specifying a second level of objects to include in the fetch. For example, if our Address entities had a relationship to a postal code lookup table that contained the city and state, we could change the NSArray creation line to the following:

```
NSArray *relationshipKeys = [NSArray arrayWithObject:@"addresses",
  @"addresses.postalCode", nil];
```

That would cause Core Data to retrieve two levels of relationships as faults. In addition, this call does check for duplication before executing the requests and thereby can be used safely when mixing keypaths. In other words, the postalCode relationship, which is probably many-to-many, will not be retrieved more than once.

NSFetchRequest and Disk Access

Every time an NSFetchRequest is executed, it hits the disk. This is an important point to keep in mind when we are working with NSManaged-Object objects. If we are doing joins, adding objects to a relationship, and so on, it might seem easier and cleaner to perform an NSFetchRequest to check to see whether the object is already in the relationship or a similar function, but that can hurt performance significantly. Even if we have all the relevant objects in memory, an NSFetchRequest is still going to hit the disk. It is far more efficient for us to use that NSPredicate against a collection that is already in memory.

We have seen in this section that with a SQLite persistent store, we have a lot of control over how our data is loaded into memory. We can tailor the load to fit our exacting needs. All of these options can be a bit overwhelming, but there is one good rule of thumb. Try to load *only* the data you need at that moment in one pass. Every fetch request can take quite a bit of time, and since they are normally performed on the main thread, they can damage the user experience of your application.

6.4 Faulting

Firing faults individually is one of the most common, if not the most common, cause for the poor performance of Core Data applications. Faults are a double-edged sword that can make great improvements to the speed and performance of our applications or can drag the performance down to the depths of the unusable. The single most valuable performance improvements we can make to a Core Data application is to make sure we are fetching only the data we need when we need it. If we fetch too little, then our application will feel unresponsive. If we

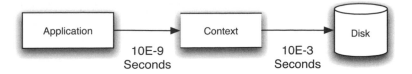

Figure 6.3: ACCESS PERFORMANCE

fetch too much, then our application will stall with the famous Spinning Beach Ball of Death.

Orders of Magnitude

Disk access is significantly slower than accessing memory. The times measured for each is *six orders of magnitude* different. This translates into disk access being roughly 1 million times slower than accessing data that is stored in memory, as illustrated in Figure 6.3.

Although the actual retrieval times are closer to a few thousand times slower, the point is still clear. Avoid accessing the disk if possible. However, when we have no choice but to access the disk, attempt to get everything we need in one pass. Repeated small requests to the disk are significantly slower than one larger request.

Prefetching

In Section 6.3, *Fetching*, on page 98, we reviewed the different ways that we can retrieve the data from disk. To expand on that, consider each request you make from the NSManagedObjectContext and try to retrieve all the data in one request that the user is going to want to view. For example, if the user is going to be editing a user record, load that user and all its relationships at once. This will be significantly faster than grabbing the Person entity and then going back to grab three Address entities, then two Phone entities, and so on. Use the relationship prefetching option of NSFetchRequest to grab all of them at once.

If we can predict what the user is going to want to see and load it ahead of their request, the overall user experience will be vastly improved. As we are developing our applications, we need to look at each window, view, or sheet and ask, "What information will this part present?" and make sure that all of that information is either already in memory or loaded at once. Having said that, we need to balance this with information overload, as discussed in Section 6.5, *Access Patterns*, on page 106.

Warming Up the Cache

As we discussed in Section 6.3, *Fetching*, on page 98, it is possible to preload the data into the cache so that it is in memory when we need it. The easiest way to perform this is to execute a full fetch on a background thread. For example, on launch of our recipe application, we could launch a background thread to retrieve all the Recipe entities. This would allow us to fill the cache with the Recipe entities that we know are going to be presented to the user. This would allow the main thread to grab those recipes from the cache instead of the disk and give the user a smoother-running application in the process. The magic behind this is based on how the NSPersistentCoordinator works. Whenever any request on any thread is performed, the data is held in the NSPersistentStoreCoordinator as part of its cache. When another request is made, no matter what thread it came from, for that same data it is retrieved from the cache instead of requiring another hit to the disk.

Saving

The numbers discussed in Section 6.4, *Orders of Magnitude*, on the previous page also apply to writing the data back out to the disk. In fact, writing to the disk is even slower than reading from it. Therefore, it is more efficient for us to save data back out to disk in batches. Saving after every record change will cause our entire application to feel sluggish to the user. Likewise, doing a huge write while the application is attempting to exit will give the appearance that our application has stopped responding and risks data loss.

As with most things when it comes to performance tuning, be aware of your saves and how much data, or how frequently, you are saving data. Try to do saves during logical pauses in the application flow.

Deleting

It may come as a surprise, but deleting an object can cause a performance issue. Let's review the data model from Chapter 5, *Versioning and Migration*, on page 67. Imagine that in this later version of our application we want to delete a recipe from the repository. When we delete the recipe, we have a cascade rule set up to delete all the associated RecipeIngredient entities as well. We also need to touch the

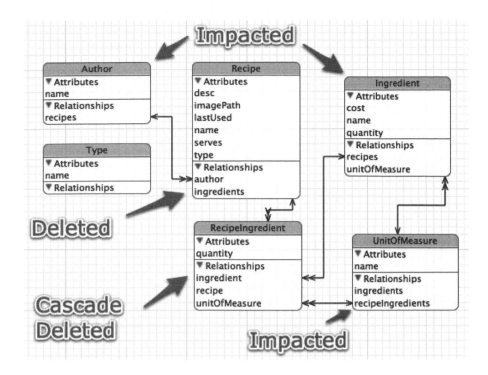

Figure 6.4: IMPACTS OF DELETING A RECIPE

Author entity, Ingredient entity, and UnitOfMeasure entity, as shown in Figure 6.4.

It is obvious why we need to touch the RecipeIngredient entity, but why do we need to access all the others? This is because of the relationships between the entities. For each relationship, we need to validate the relationship after the delete and confirm that there are no dangling references. If these objects are not currently in memory, then the NSManagedObjectContext must retrieve them from the disk to accomplish all of this.

Therefore, when we are doing deletes, especially large deletes, it can be a performance improvement to fetch all the relationships prior to the delete.

Faulting and Disk Access

Firing a fault does not always mean that the data is going to be read from disk. Depending on how we have requested the data in the first place or what happened earlier in the NSManagedObject object's life span, it is quite possible that the data will be loaded from cache instead.

Likewise, faulting an NSManagedObject does not guarantee that it will be written back out to disk nor does it guarantee that it will be removed from the cache. If the object has no changes, then there is nothing to write to disk, and it is quite possible that it will remain in the cache for an unknown period of time.

Easily one of the best ways to check to see whether the firing of a fault is in fact causing disk access is to monitor our application with instruments. By using the Core Data template, we can use the "cache miss" instrument to check for disk hits. If we are getting far more calls to the disk than expected, then we need to consider refactoring the code.

6.5 Access Patterns

Improving performance within Core Data is not necessarily only about the repository and order of loading the data. There are a number of things that we can do within the user interface to help performance as well.

Searching

Searching the repository can be absolute murder on performance. Whether we are searching at the request of the user or we are performing a search in the background, we need to be very careful to avoid impacting the performance of our application.

Order Is Important

Just like any conditional, the order of the logic is important. Simple equality is faster than inclusions such as in, contains, and so on. When building the predicate, try to order the logic from left to right, simple to complex. This will allow Core Data to fail quickly and improve the search performance.

Unicode and Regular Expressions

Unicode is very expensive to work with when we are searching. As suggested earlier in Section 6.2, *Search Only Properties*, on page 96, try to avoid searching against Unicode directly. It is cheaper to keep a derived value that strips off the Unicode than it is to do frequent searches against the Unicode text.

Likewise, regular expressions are expensive. If a situation calls for one, try to put it at the far right end of the NSPredicate, as discussed in Section 6.5, *Order Is Important*, on the preceding page.

Limit Queries Across Relationships

Searching across objects that are joined by a relationship can be very expensive for searching. Although it is impressive to search against person.address.postalCode.city, it may not be the most efficient way to solve the problem. Consider reversing the query or breaking it down into several smaller queries to reduce the complexity of the underlying SQL. When we are working with a SQLite back end, all of our NSPredicate calls turn into SQL before hitting the database. The less complex that SQL is, the faster it will run. It may very well be faster to get an NSArray of all the Address objects within a specific city and then perform the rest of the query against that NSArray than it would be to traverse three relationships in one call.

Information Overload

A busy user interface is more than just a poor user experience; it also impacts the performance of the application. When we display a large amount of data on the screen, we must keep that information in memory, which in turn means we must load a large amount of data from disk all in one go. It is far better to break an application user interface up into consumable chunks of information than it is to try to display every last bit on the screen at once.

The careful use of tabs, sheets, and panels can improve the feel of a user interface, and that will in turn improve the performance. By splitting the user interface into smaller pieces, we have finer-grained control over what data gets loaded when, and we can reduce our disk access to manageable chunks.

Keep it simple.

Chapter 7

Spotlight, Quick Look, and Core Data

Developing for Mac OS X is about functionality meeting quality. When our applications have either without the other, we leave our users wanting more. They may not be able to define it, but "something" will be missing. Spotlight and Quick Look integration are two of those things that users don't look for when trying a new application but are pleasantly surprised by them when they stumble upon them. Surprisingly, not a lot of developers handle this integration. Perhaps it is because Spotlight does not get along with Core Data very well. Perhaps the feature is too new. But one thing is for certain—integrating with Spotlight is the right move going forward. Spotlight is here to stay, and users will be using it more often and in more creative ways.

Unfortunately, for technical reasons, Spotlight and Core Data are at odds with each other. Spotlight works on the metadata of individual files, and Core Data stores everything in a single file. Because Spotlight is designed to work with the metadata of a file to discover things about the file, it will not work very well with a single file design such as Core Data. When Tiger was first released, there were a number of applications (such as Entourage) that, because of their single file design, did not play nicely with Spotlight. In fact, Apple rearchitected Mail for that reason.

The incompatibility between Spotlight and Core Data is corrected in Snow Leopard but unfortunately it's Snow Leopard only and not backward compatible with plain old vanilla Leopard. How? It's in a manner that is very similar to the solution described in this chapter.

Should I Just Use Separate Files?

Throughout this book, the application we are designing uses a single Core Data file. This is done for the sake of clarity and focus on Core Data. Depending on the application that is being designed, it is highly likely that it will be document based, and therefore it would be appropriate to have one Core Data repository per document. In that situation, Spotlight and Quick Look can be a lot easier to integrate.

However, for applications that are not document based, then it is preferable to use a single Core Data repository as opposed to individual files. Although individual files will make Spotlight easier to work with, it would be the tail wagging the dog. The main focus of object persistence (in other words, data files) is to quickly and easily access the data in a logical and reproducible manner. Core Data solves all those problems quite neatly with the unfortunately minor side effect of not being fully compatible with Spotlight.

In this chapter, we will integrate Spotlight into our recipes application. Once we are done, our users will be able to search for *Pot Roast* and find it in our application. In addition, when they select that search result, our application will not only open but open to Pot Roast. While we are solving the Spotlight issue, we are also going to take a look at Quick Look. Although on the surface these two technologies appear to be completely different, they are handled in a very similar fashion by Mac OS X and the Finder. And although it is not 100 percent appropriate for our sample application (since we have only a single data file and that data file is hidden away in the Library/Application Support directory), it is very useful to understand how Quick Look works for document-based Core Data applications because it makes them easier to find in Finder, Spotlight, Time Machine, Mail, and many other applications. Lastly, Quick Look and Spotlight integrate rather well together. If our users activate Quick Look on a Spotlight result, we want them to see information about the recipe, not a picture of a generic file.

7.1 Integrating with Spotlight

The issue, as mentioned, is one of multiple files. Ideally, for our recipe application, we want one Spotlight "record" for each recipe in our Core Data repository. For Spotlight to work properly, we would need one file on the disk for each recipe along with its associated metadata. Therefore, to make Spotlight happy, we will do exactly that. However, since all our data is being stored in a Core Data repository, there is no reason to store any data in these files. These additional files exist purely for Spotlight (and Quick Look) to utilize. Since Spotlight does not need any data in the files to work (it just needs metadata), we will create very simple files and link them back to our Core Data repository.

The other gotcha with Spotlight is that the importer needs to be as fast as possible. What might be acceptable for processing one file or ten files is not going to fly when Spotlight has to chug through thousands of files. Since the same importer that we are writing for use inside our application could potentially be used in a server situation, it needs to be as fast as we can make it. Therefore, we will cheat a bit. Instead of looking up the metadata in our Core Data repository upon request from Spotlight, we will instead store that metadata in the files we are creating for Spotlight. That way, our importer has to touch the metadata files only and does not need to initialize the entire Core Data "stack" (NSManagedObjectContext, NSPersistentStoreCoordinator, and NSManagedObjectModel).

Creating the Metadata Files

We first need to produce and update the metadata files on the fly. To keep them as simple as possible, we will just use plist files as opposed to a binary representation or some other format. Since NSDictionary understands plist files, it will reduce the amount of overhead we have for loading and saving the files.

To begin with, we will create our first NSManagedObject subclass. This subclass will handle producing the NSDictionary that will contain all the metadata. Since we are creating a subclass, we might as well implement some of the properties we will be using to reduce the code complexity and make it easier to maintain.

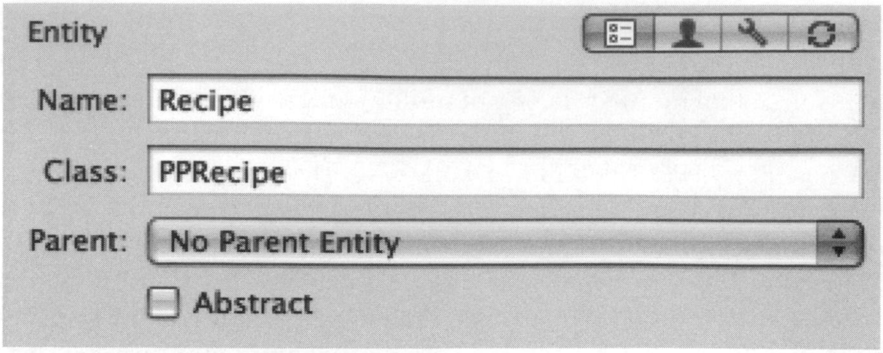

Figure 7.1: CHANGING THE ENTITY'S CLASS

Therefore, our header file will look as follows:

`Spotlight/PPRecipe.h`

```
#import <Cocoa/Cocoa.h>

extern NSString *kPPImagePath;
extern NSString *kPPObjectID;
extern NSString *kPPServes;

@interface PPRecipe : NSManagedObject {

}

@property (assign) NSString *desc;
@property (assign) NSString *name;
@property (assign) NSString *type;
@property (assign) NSManagedObject *author;
@property (assign) NSDate *lastUsed;

- (NSDictionary*)metadata;
- (NSString*)metadataFilename;

@end
```

We need to make sure that we change the class setting in the latest data model so that Core Data will use our subclass rather than the default NSManagedObject. See Figure 7.1.

Implementing the Metadata Method

The goal of this metadata file is to contain just enough information to populate Spotlight and Quick Look but not too much information that the files become large and cumbersome. We always have to pretend that there will be thousands of these files (even if in reality that would be impractical), and we do not want to impact the user's performance or their hard drive capacity. For our metadata files, we really need only the following information:

- The name of the recipe
- The number of people it serves
- The image for the recipe
- The last time it was served
- The description of how to prepare it

Most of that list is very light—just text. However, the image is probably too large to cram into the plist file, especially since we cannot be sure how large those files will be. In addition, it would complicate the file format by including binary data. Therefore, we will put in its path instead of the actual image. Since the image is stored on disk anyway, we can just access that copy.

In addition to this list, we need to add one more item that is not user facing. We want a way to link back to the recipe record in our Core Data repository so that if the user tries to open the metadata file, it will instead open our application and select the correct record. To do this, we will use the NSManagedObjectID of the recipe and store its URIRepresentation (which is actually an NSURL) as a string in the metadata.

`Spotlight/PPRecipe.m`

```
- (NSDictionary*)metadata;
{
  NSMutableDictionary *metadataDict = [NSMutableDictionary dictionary];

  [metadataDict setValue:[self name]
              forKey:(id)kMDItemTitle];
  [metadataDict setValue:[self desc]
              forKey:(id)kMDItemTextContent];
  [metadataDict setValue:[[self author] valueForKey:@"name"]
              forKey:(id)kMDItemAuthors];
  [metadataDict setValue:[self valueForKey:@"imagePath"]
              forKey:kPPImagePath];
  [metadataDict setValue:[self lastUsed] forKey:(id)kMDItemLastUsedDate];
  [metadataDict setValue:[self valueForKey:@"serves"] forKey:kPPServes];
  [metadataDict setValue:[NSString stringWithFormat:@"Recipe: %@", [self name]]
              forKey:(id)kMDItemDisplayName];
  [metadataDict setValue:[[[self objectID] URIRepresentation] absoluteString]
              forKey:kPPObjectID];
  return metadataDict;
}
```

Implementing the metadataName Method

Because we want users to be able to view the actual metadata files in
the Finder, the filenames should represent the recipe rather than an
abstract name. Therefore, we will use the name attribute of the recipe
itself as the filename:

Spotlight/PPRecipe.m

```
- (NSString*)metadataFilename;
{
  return [[self name] stringByAppendingPathExtension:@"grokkingrecipe"];
}
```

Generating and Updating the Metadata Files

Now that we have an implementation for generating the metadata per
recipe, we need to add the ability to populate these files and keep them
up-to-date. Ideally, we want to refresh the metadata files every time
that the NSManagedObjectContext is saved. To do this, we will add a new
-save: method to our AppDelegate and route all of our saves through it:

Spotlight/AppDelegate.m

```
- (BOOL)save:(NSError**)error;
{
  NSManagedObjectContext *moc = [self managedObjectContext];
  if (!moc) return YES;

  if (![moc hasChanges]) return YES;

  //Grab a reference to all of the objects we will need to work with
  NSSet *deleted = [moc deletedObjects];
  NSMutableSet *deletedPaths = [NSMutableSet set];
  for (NSManagedObject *object in deleted) {
    if (![object isKindOfClass:[PPRecipe class]]) continue;
    [deletedPaths addObject:[object valueForKey:@"metadataFilename"]];
  }

  NSMutableSet *updated = [NSMutableSet setWithSet:[moc insertedObjects]];
  [updated unionSet:[moc updatedObjects]];

  //Save the context
  if (![moc save:error]) {
    return NO;
  }
  return [self updateMetadataForObjects:updated
                    andDeletedObjects:deletedPaths
                              error:error];
}
```

In this new -save: method, we are doing a couple of things before calling save on the NSManagedObjectContext. Since the NSManagedObjectContext knows what objects have been deleted, updated, or inserted, we want to grab a reference to that information before the -save: occurs. Once the -save: is complete, that information is no longer available. Therefore, we grab a reference to the NSSet of deleted objects, updated objects, and inserted objects. Because the deleted objects will be, well, deleted once the -save: is performed, we want to extract the information we care about beforehand. Therefore, we loop over the deleted objects looking for Recipe instances. Whenever we find one, we extract its metadataFilename and store it in a new NSMutableSet. In addition, since we will be doing the same thing to the inserted and the updated objects, we merge them into one set. Once we have that information, we go ahead and save the context. If the save fails, we just abort and let the calling code handle the error. When the save is successful, it is time to update the metadata.

Spotlight/AppDelegate.m

```
if ((!updatedObjects || ![updatedObjects count]) &&
    (!deletedObjects || ![deletedObjects count])) return YES;

NSString *path = [self metadataFolder:error];
if (!path) return NO;

BOOL directory = NO;

NSFileManager *fileManager = [NSFileManager defaultManager];
if (![fileManager fileExistsAtPath:path isDirectory:&directory]) {
  if (![fileManager createDirectoryAtPath:path
              withIntermediateDirectories:YES
                               attributes:nil
                                    error:error]) {
    return NO;
  }
  directory = YES;
}
if (!directory) {
  NSMutableDictionary *errorDict = [NSMutableDictionary dictionary];
  NSString *msg = NSLocalizedString(@"File in place of metadata directory",
    @"metadata directory is a file error description");
  [errorDict setValue:msg forKey:NSLocalizedDescriptionKey];
  *error = [NSError errorWithDomain:@"pragprog" code:1001 userInfo:errorDict];
  return NO;
}
```

In the habit of assuming nothing, we first check to make sure that there is something to update or delete. Once we are past that check, we next need to confirm that the cache directory is in place and either our metadata directory is in place or we can create it. If any of this fails, we update the NSError object and return.

`Spotlight/AppDelegate.m`

```
NSString *filePath = nil;
if (deletedObjects && [deletedObjects count]) {
  for (NSString *filename in deletedObjects) {
    filePath = [path stringByAppendingPathComponent:filename];
    if (![fileManager fileExistsAtPath:filePath]) continue;
    if (![fileManager removeItemAtPath:filePath error:error]) return NO;
  }
}
```

The next part of updating the metadata is to remove any files that are no longer appropriate. Therefore, if the passed-in deletedObjects set contains any objects, we need to loop over it. Since we know that the name of the metadata file is stored in the deletedObjects variable, we append it to the metadata directory path and check for the existence of the file. If it exists, we delete it.[1] If we run into an issue deleting the file, then we abort the update and let the calling method handle the error.

`Spotlight/AppDelegate.m`

```
if (!updatedObjects || ![updatedObjects count]) return YES;

NSNumber *_YES = [NSNumber numberWithBool:YES];
NSDictionary *attributesDictionary = [NSDictionary
                                dictionaryWithObject:_YES
                                forKey:NSFileExtensionHidden];

for (NSString *filename in updatedObjects) {
  if (![object isKindOfClass:[PPRecipe class]]) continue;
  PPRecipe *recipe = (PPRecipe*)object;
  NSDictionary *metadata = [recipe metadata];
  filePath = [recipe metadataFilename];
  filePath = [path stringByAppendingPathComponent:filePath];
  [metadata writeToFile:filePath atomically:YES];
  [fileManager changeFileAttributes:attributesDictionary atPath:filePath];
}

return YES;
```

The last part of updating the metadata files is to process existing or new recipes. As with the deleted objects earlier, we first check to see whether there are any objects to update, and if there are not, we are

---

1. It may be possible that a recipe got created and deleted without ever being saved to disk. It's unlikely, but why take chances?

done and successful. If there are new or updated objects, then we again loop through the NSSet looking for PPRecipe entities. For each recipe that we find, we request its metadata NSDictionary object from the metadata method we created earlier. Using that NSDictionary along with the metadataFilename method, we write the NSDictionary to disk. For one last bit of polish, we update the attributes on the newly created (or updated) file and tell it to hide its file extension. This will give us the cleanest appearance when viewed inside the Finder.

Now that the -save: method has been written, we need to route all the -save: calls that exist to call this method instead of calling -save: directly on the NSManagedObjectContext. Currently, this requires modifying both the -(NSApplicationTerminateReply)applicationShouldTerminate: method and the -(IBAction)saveAction: method. In each case, we just need to change the following:

```
[[self managedObjectContext] save:&error]
```

to a message to the -save: method on the AppDelegate itself:

```
[self save:&error];
```

There is one last situation we need to handle. If we have existing users and are adding the Spotlight integration after v1.0, we need some way to bring our users up to speed. To do this, we need to add a check to the -(void)applicationDidFinishLaunching: method. If the metadata directory does not exist, then we need to do a full push of all the metadata in the persistent store.

`Spotlight/AppDelegate.m`

```
NSError *error = nil;
NSString *path = [self metadataFolder:&error];
if (!path) {
  NSLog(@"%@:%s Error resolving cache path: %@", [self class], _cmd, error);
  return;
}
if ([[NSFileManager defaultManager] fileExistsAtPath:path]) return;

NSManagedObjectContext *moc = [self managedObjectContext];
NSFetchRequest *request = [[[NSFetchRequest alloc] init] autorelease];
[request setEntity:[NSEntityDescription entityForName:@"Recipe"
                              inManagedObjectContext:moc]];

NSSet *recipes = [NSSet setWithArray:[moc executeFetchRequest:request
                                                        error:&error]];
if (error) {
  NSLog(@"%@:%s Error: %@", [self class], _cmd, error);
  return;
}
```

```
[self updateMetadataForObjects:recipes andDeletedObjects:nil error:&error];
if (error) {
  NSLog(@"%@:%s Error: %@", [self class], _cmd, error);
  return;
}
```

Here we are looking for the metadata cache directory, and if it does not exist, then we fetch every recipe entity in the persistent store and pass the NSSet to our metadata building method. This will also protect us from users who like to periodically delete their cache directory. This method calls the -metadataFolder method to determine where the metadata should be stored.

Spotlight/AppDelegate.m

```
- (NSString*)metadataFolder:(NSError**)error
{
  NSString *path = [NSSearchPathForDirectoriesInDomains(NSCachesDirectory,
                                               NSUserDomainMask, YES)
                    lastObject];
  if (!path) {
    NSMutableDictionary *errorDict = [NSMutableDictionary dictionary];
    [errorDict setValue:NSLocalizedString(@"Failed to locate caches directory",
                              @"caches directory error description")
            forKey:NSLocalizedDescriptionKey];
    *error = [NSError errorWithDomain:@"pragprog" code:1000 userInfo:errorDict];
    return nil;
  }
  path = [path stringByAppendingPathComponent:@"Metadata"];
  path = [path stringByAppendingPathComponent:@"GrokkingRecipes"];
  return path;
}
```

In the -metadataFolder, we first request a list of the cache directories from the NSSearchPathForDirectoiesInDomain method and append the path components Metadata and GrokkingRecipes to it. We do not check to see whether the path exists at this point but instead let our caller decide how to handle that.

Creating the Spotlight Importer

Now that we have some metadata to work with, it is time to build the Spotlight importer. To start off this part of the application, we need to first address UTIs.

Uniform Type Identifiers (UTIs)

Both Spotlight and Quick Look use UTIs rather than filename extensions to connect files on disk with (Spotlight) importers and (Quick Look) generators. A UTI is a unique string that identifies the type of data stored in a given file. It is recommended that UTIs identify the company and application that created the data file, and like bundle identifiers, a reverse domain name is ideal for this purpose.[2] Since our application uses com.pragprog.grokkingrecipes as its unique bundle identifier, we will use the same UTI as the value of the LSItemContentTypes to identify the files.

`Spotlight/Info.plist`

```
<key>CFBundleDocumentTypes</key>
<array>
        <dict>
                <key>CFBundleTypeExtensions</key>
                <array>
                        <string>grokkingrecipe</string>
                </array>
                <key>CFBundleTypeIconFile</key>
                <string>book.icns</string>
                <key>CFBundleTypeName</key>
                <string>Grokking Recipe</string>
                <key>CFBundleTypeRole</key>
                <string>Editor</string>
                <key>LSItemContentTypes</key>
                <array>
                        <string>com.pragprog.grokkingrecipe</string>
                </array>
                <key>NSPersistentStoreTypeKey</key>
                <string>XML</string>
        </dict>
</array>
```

The UTExportedTypeDeclarations section is probably very familiar. Xcode generates it to describe any file that is handled by the application being built. The one difference is that, instead of defining a file extension (like .txt), we are defining a UTI that is being handled by our application. Since this UTI is unknown by the system, we need to describe it, again in our Info.plist file:

`Spotlight/Info.plist`

```
<key>UTExportedTypeDeclarations</key>
<array>
        <dict>
                <key>UTTypeConformsTo</key>
                <array>
                        <string>public.data</string>
                        <string>public.content</string>
                </array>
                <key>UTTypeDescription</key>
```

---

2. It should be noted that bundle identifiers are in fact UTIs themselves.

```
            <string>Grokking Recipe</string>
            <key>UTTypeIdentifier</key>
            <string>com.pragprog.grokkingrecipe</string>
            <key>UTTypeTagSpecification</key>
            <dict>
                    <key>public.filename-extension</key>
                    <string>grokkingrecipe</string>
            </dict>
        </dict>
    </array>
```

This key describes exporting our UTI and tells Mac OS X how to link it to different file extensions. In addition, this section describes the data to Mac OS X, telling the OS a descriptive name for the data type and where in the UTI tree it fits.[3]

Xcode Subproject

Our Spotlight importer is actually its own application. Xcode handles this by having a separate project for the importer.[4] Since we want to include the importer as part of our primary application and we do not want to have to remember to rebuild the subproject every time we build our main project, we will set it up as a dependent or subproject within our primary project. To do this, we start with creating a project in Xcode and selecting the Spotlight importer, as shown in Figure 7.2, on the next page. We want to save this project in a directory inside our primary recipe project. Don't be too clever. Give the subproject an obvious name like SpotlightPlugin, and include it with the Spotlight example project. To make Xcode build this plug-in every time we build the main project, we need to link the two together. This is accomplished with the following steps:

1. Drag the subproject into the main project. See Figure 7.3, on the facing page.

2. Open the target in the main project, and select the General tab.

3. Add the subproject as a dependency.

4. Add a new copy phase to the main project's target, and set its destination to wrapper and path to Contents/Library/Spotlight.

---

3. For more information on UTIs, I suggest reviewing http://developer.apple.com/documentation/Carbon/Conceptual/understanding_utis/understand_utis_intro/chapter_1_section_1.html#//apple_ref/doc/uid/TP40001319-CH201-SW1.

4. It is actually possible to include the plug-in as part of the main application project, but I have found that to be a complete mess and more hassle than it is worth.

Figure 7.2: SELECT THE SPOTLIGHT TEMPLATE.

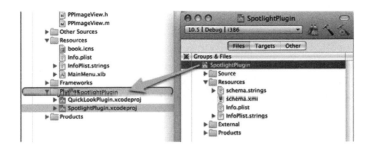

Figure 7.3: DRAG THE SUBPROJECT INTO THE MAIN PROJECT.

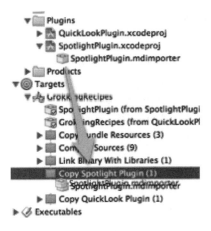

Figure 7.4: DRAG THE PLUG-IN INTO ITS BUILD PHASE.

5. Drag the Spotlight plug-in into the new build phase. See Figure 7.4, on the previous page.

Now, whenever we clean or build the main project, the subproject will be cleaned/built. This will also allow the subproject to be built with the same settings as the primary project.

Linking the Spotlight Importer to the UTI

With our Spotlight importer subproject in place, it is time to link the importer to the UTI for our metadata files. To do this, we need to update the Info.plist of our Spotlight subproject to let the operating system know which UTIs this importer handles.

```
<array>
  <dict>
    <key>CFBundleTypeRole</key>
    <string>MDImporter</string>
    <key>LSItemContentTypes</key>
    <array>
      <string>com.pragprog.grokkingrecipe</string>
    </array>
  </dict>
</array>
```

Here, we are defining our plug-in as having an MDImporter role, and the list of UTIs contains just the one for our metadata file. With this change, Mac OS X will know to use this importer to retrieve the information for our metadata files.

Building the Spotlight Importer

Now that everything is connected, it is time to build the importer itself. Fortunately, this is the easiest and shortest part of the entire process. The Spotlight template created the main.m file that we will be using, and it contains all the boilerplate code for us. The only code we need to write for the importer is in the GetMetadataForFile.m file. The template generates a GetMetadataForFile.c file, and that file will not accept any Objective-C code. Since I prefer Objective-C over straight C, the first thing I did was rename the .c file to an .m file. This tells Xcode to compile it as Objective-C rather than C. Since we will be using Foundation APIs, we need to include Foundation.framework as well.

Spotlight/SpotlightPlugin/GetMetadataForFile.m

```
#include <CoreFoundation/CoreFoundation.h>
#include <CoreServices/CoreServices.h>

#import <Foundation/Foundation.h>
```

```
Boolean GetMetadataForFile(void* thisInterface,
                           CFMutableDictionaryRef attributes,
                           CFStringRef contentTypeUTI,
                           CFStringRef pathToFile)
{
  NSAutoreleasePool *pool = [[NSAutoreleasePool alloc] init];
  NSDictionary *metadata;
  metadata = [NSDictionary dictionaryWithContentsOfFile:(NSString*)pathToFile];
  for (NSString *key in [metadata allKeys]) {
    [(id)attributes setObject:[metadata objectForKey:key] forKey:key];
  }
  [pool release], pool = nil;
  return TRUE;
}
```

The actual code for the importer is almost laughable. We are simply loading the metadata file back into an NSDictionary, looping over the keys using the allKeys method, and adding each associated value to the passed-in CFMutableDictionaryRef. Once we are done with the NSDictionary, we return TRUE and are done. Since we are running inside a C function, we need to wrap the entire procedure in an NSAutoreleasePool so that we are not leaking any memory.

Testing the Spotlight Importer

There are a couple of ways to test the importer to make sure that everything is working properly. The first thing we need to do is to generate the metadata files. We can do this by running our application. Once the metadata files are created, we can test the importer.

We can get a lot of information about our importer directly on the command line. Included with Mac OS X is a command-line tool called mdimport. A quick review of the man page will reveal that there are three switches for this command that are of immediate use. First, we need to tell Spotlight to load our importer:

```
mdimport -r ${path to our project}/build/Debug/GrokkingRecipes.app/
  Contents/Library/Spotlight/SpotlightPlugin.mdimporter
```

Once Spotlight is aware of our importer, we can start querying it, again from the command line using the mdimport command:

```
cd ~/Library/Caches/Metadata/GrokkingRecipes
mdimport -d2 Test.grokkingrecipe
```

We can change the debug level from 1 to 4 to display different quantities of information about the metadata file. However, level 2 will tell us that the importer is working and give us a basic summary of the data contained inside the file.

Figure 7.5: THE POT ROAST RECIPE IN SPOTLIGHT

The other way to test the importer is to just search for one of our recipes! Click the spotlight magnifying glass in the upper-right corner, and enter the name of one of the recipes, as in Figure 7.5. But what happens when we try to open this file?

Accepting Metadata Files

Since we linked our metadata files to the primary application, Mac OS X will attempt to open our application and pass the file to us. However, we have no way of handling that yet.

```
Spotlight/AppDelegate.m
- (BOOL)application:(NSApplication*)theApplication
         openFile:(NSString*)filename
{
  NSDictionary *metadata = [NSDictionary dictionaryWithContentsOfFile:filename];
  NSString *objectIDString = [metadata valueForKey:(id)kPPObjectID];
  NSURL *objectURI = [NSURL URLWithString:objectIDString];

  NSPersistentStoreCoordinator *coordinator;
  coordinator = [[self managedObjectContext] persistentStoreCoordinator];

  NSManagedObjectID *objectID;
  objectID = [coordinator managedObjectIDForURIRepresentation:objectURI];

  NSManagedObject *recipe = [[self managedObjectContext] objectWithID:objectID];
  if (!recipe) return NO;

  [self performSelector:@selector(selectRecipe:)
            withObject:recipe
            afterDelay:0.01];

  return YES;
}
```

In our application delegate, we need to add the method -(BOOL)application:openFile: that will be called when the operating system attempts to open one of our metadata files. In that method, we will load the metadata file into an NSDictionary and retrieve the URIRepresentation of the NSManagedObjectID. With the NSManagedObjectID in hand, we can load the represented Recipe entity and display it to the user. Since we want to return from this method as quickly as possible (since the operating system is waiting on an answer), we will display the recipe *after* we return from this method. To do that, we wrap the call to display the recipe in a -(void)performSelector:withObject:afterDelay, which will pass the recipe to the -(void)selectRecipe: method almost immediately after this method returns.

The -(void)selectRecipe: method simply sets the selectedObjects on the recipe's NSArrayController to the passed-in Recipe, which will then be reflected in the UI.

Spotlight/AppDelegate.m
```
- (void)selectRecipe:(NSManagedObject*)recipe;
{
    [recipeArrayController setSelectedObjects:[NSArray arrayWithObject:recipe]];
}
```

With that code in place, we can select a recipe from Spotlight, and our application will open with the correct recipe selected. The first part of our OS integration is now in place.

7.2 Integrating with Quick Look

There are two different ways to implement Quick Look. The application can generate images as part of the data bundle, or a generator can be written that will generate the images on the fly. Storing images with the data is viable only if the data is stored in a bundle similar to the way that Pages or Numbers does. When the data is stored in a flat file, like our metadata files, then a generator is the only way to integrate with Quick Look. Fortunately, writing a Quick Look generator is only slightly more complicated than a Spotlight importer.

Adding the Subproject

Just like the Spotlight importer, the Quick Look generator is created within its own subproject.

▼ 📁 Plugins
    ▼ 🅰 QuickLookPlugin.xcodeproj
        📦 GrokkingRecipes.qlgenerator
    ▼ 🅰 SpotlightPlugin.xcodeproj
        📦 SpotlightPlugin.mdimporter
  ▶ 📁 Products
▼ ◎ Targets
    ▼ 🔧 GrokkingRecipes
        📦 SpotlightPlugin (from SpotlightPlugin.xcodeproj)
        📦 GrokkingRecipes (from QuickLookPlugin.xcodeproj)
    ▶ 🗄 Copy Bundle Resources (3)
    ▶ 🗄 Compile Sources (9)
    ▶ 🗄 Link Binary With Libraries (1)
    ▼ 🗄 Copy Spotlight Plugin (1)
        📦 SpotlightPlugin.mdimporter
    ▼ 🗄 Copy QuickLook Plugin (1)
        📦 GrokkingRecipes.qlgenerator

Figure 7.6: THE XCODE PROJECT TREE WITH ALL PLUG-INS ADDED

Like the Spotlight importer subproject we added earlier, we need to perform the following steps:

1. Create a subproject under our recipes project. Again, I named mine the very clever name of QuickLookPlugin.
2. Drag the project into the main project, and flag it as a dependency.
3. Add a new copy phase to the main project's target, and set its destination to wrapper and path to Contents/Library/QuickLook.
4. Drag the Quick Look plug-in into the new build phase.

If any of these steps are confusing, please see Section 7.1, *Xcode Subproject*, on page 120. Once the Quick Look subproject has been added, the main project's tree should look similar to Figure 7.6.

Once the subproject has been set up properly, we will go ahead and rename the two .c files to .m files so that we can use Objective-C inside them. We need to also add Foundation.framework to the subproject so that we can utilize the Foundation APIs.

Unlike Spotlight, Quick Look has two components. There is a thumbnail generation and a preview generation. The thumbnail is used by the

Finder both in place of a standard file icon and in Cover Flow. The pre-view is used when Quick Look is invoked in Finder, Mail, and so on. Therefore, the Quick Look template creates two .c (now .m) files, one for each. We will tackle the thumbnail file first.

Generating the Quick Look Thumbnail

The file GenerateThumbnailForURL.m has one function inside it that is called by the Quick Look manager (part of the operating system). This function expects that we will be populating the QLThumbnailRequestRef and returning the OSStatus of noErr. Based on the documentation for Quick Look, even if we suffer a complete failure inside of our plug-in, we should always return noErr.

As you can probably guess, our thumbnail generation code is going to be very simple. Since we already have an image included with each recipe, we are simply going to pass that image back whenever it is requested.

Spotlight/QuickLookPlugin/GenerateThumbnailForURL.m

```
OSStatus GenerateThumbnailForURL(void *thisInterface,
                                 QLThumbnailRequestRef thumbnail,
                                 CFURLRef url,
                                 CFStringRef contentTypeUTI,
                                 CFDictionaryRef options,
                                 CGSize maxSize)
{
  NSAutoreleasePool *pool = [[NSAutoreleasePool alloc] init];
  @try {
    NSDictionary *metadata;
    metadata = [NSDictionary dictionaryWithContentsOfURL:(NSURL*)url];
    NSString *pathToImage = [metadata valueForKey:@"kPPImagePath"];
    if (!pathToImage) {
      //No image available
      return noErr;
    }
    NSData *imageData = [NSData dataWithContentsOfFile:pathToImage];
    if (!imageData) {
      //Unable to load the data for some reason.
      return noErr;
    }

    QLThumbnailRequestSetImageWithData(thumbnail, (CFDataRef)imageData, NULL);
  } @finally {
    [pool release], pool = nil;
  }
  return noErr;
}
```

Figure 7.7: BASIC QUICK LOOK PREVIEW

In this method, we are again retrieving the metadata file and loading it into an NSDictionary. From that dictionary we are retrieving the path to the image for the recipe and loading the image into an NSData object. From there, we then call the QLThumbnailRequestSetImageWith-Data(QLThumbnailRequestRef, CFDataRect, CFDictionaryRef) method, which will populate the QLThumbnailRequestRef. After that is done, we pop the NSAutoreleasePool and return noErr. From there Quick Look will use the image we have provided whenever it needs a thumbnail for the file.

Generating the Quick Look preview

The Quick Look preview is understandably more complex than generating a thumbnail image. If we do absolutely nothing for this part of Quick Look, we would still get a rather satisfying preview, as shown in Figure 7.7. But why stop there when we can do so much more?

Like the thumbnail generator in Section 7.2, *Generating the Quick Look Thumbnail*, on the preceding page, the preview generator is contained within one function call, and we are expected to populate the QLPreviewRequestRef and return noErr. Also, like the thumbnail generator, we will always return noErr no matter what happens within our function call.

Unlike the thumbnail generator, we are not going to be working with just the image for the recipe. Instead, we will generate a full HTML page that contains a large amount of information about the recipe and use that as our preview. Although it would be possible to generate the entire HTML page in code, I am rather lazy and would rather avoid that. Instead, we will be taking advantage of some XPath queries to locate the correct nodes inside a template HTML file, change the values to be appropriate for our current recipe, and use that to generate the QLPreviewRequestRef.

Spotlight/QuickLookPlugin/GeneratePreviewForURL.m

```
NSString *bundleID = @"com.pragprog.quicklook.grokkingrecipe";

OSStatus GeneratePreviewForURL(void *thisInterface,
                               QLPreviewRequestRef preview,
                               CFURLRef url,
                               CFStringRef contentTypeUTI,
                               CFDictionaryRef options)
{
  NSAutoreleasePool *pool = [[NSAutoreleasePool alloc] init];
  @try {
    NSDictionary *metadata;
    metadata = [NSDictionary dictionaryWithContentsOfURL:(NSURL*)url];
    if (!metadata) return noErr;
    NSLog(@"metadata: %@", metadata);

    NSString *imagePath = [metadata valueForKey:@"kPPImagePath"];
    NSData *imageData = [[NSData alloc] initWithContentsOfFile:imagePath];
    if (!imageData) return noErr;
```

To start with, we load the metadata dictionary like we have previously. We are also going to load the image data into an NSData object again. Assuming there are no issues with either the metadata or the image loading, the next step is to set up the options for the HTML page.

Spotlight/QuickLookPlugin/GeneratePreviewForURL.m

```
NSMutableDictionary *imageDict = [NSMutableDictionary dictionary];
[imageDict setValue:imageData
           forKey:(id)kQLPreviewPropertyAttachmentDataKey];

if (QLPreviewRequestIsCancelled(preview)) return noErr;

NSMutableDictionary *attachments = [NSMutableDictionary dictionary];
[attachments setValue:imageDict forKey:@"preview-image"];

NSMutableDictionary *properties = [NSMutableDictionary dictionary];
[properties setValue:attachments
            forKey:(id)kQLPreviewPropertyAttachmentsKey];
```

```
[properties setValue:@"text/html"
            forKey:(id)kQLPreviewPropertyMIMETypeKey];
[properties setValue:@"UTF-8"
            forKey:(id)kQLPreviewPropertyTextEncodingNameKey];
[properties setValue:@"Recipe"
            forKey:(id)kQLPreviewPropertyDisplayNameKey];
```

For Quick Look to be able to use the HTML page that we are handing to it, it requires that we describe the document to it and include any attachments it has. This helps improve the performance of the HTML rendering since it does not have to fetch any of the attachments. Therefore, in this section, we are setting up the properties for the HTML page including specifying its encoding, MIME type, and the attachments. We also give it a display name that will be used outside the HTML page.

`Spotlight/QuickLookPlugin/GeneratePreviewForURL.m`

```
NSBundle *bundle = [NSBundle bundleWithIdentifier:bundleID];
NSString *templatePath = [bundle pathForResource:@"preview" ofType:@"html"];
NSURL *templateURL = [NSURL fileURLWithPath:templatePath];

NSError *error = nil;
NSXMLDocument *template;
template = [[[NSXMLDocument alloc] initWithContentsOfURL:(NSURL*)templateURL
                                         options:NSXMLDocumentTidyHTML
                                           error:&error] autorelease];

if (!template) {
  NSLog(@"Failed to build template: %@", error);
  return noErr;
}
```

Once all the preliminaries are complete, we need to retrieve the HTML template from our bundle. Since this code is not actually being called from our bundle, we cannot just perform (NSBundle mainBundle) and get a reference to our NSBundle.[5] Instead, we have to request it by its UTI. With a reference to the bundle, we can then retrieve the path to the preview.html, which we will be using as our template. Once we have loaded the HTML file into an NSXMLDocument, it is time to substitute the placeholders in that file with real data.

`Spotlight/QuickLookPlugin/GeneratePreviewForURL.m`

```
//Updating the Title
error = nil;
NSXMLElement *element = [[template nodesForXPath:
                          @"/html/body/div/*[@id='title']"
                                        error:&error] lastObject];
```

---

5. If we tried, we would actually get a reference to /usr/bin/qlmanage instead!

```
if (!element) {
  NSLog(@"Failed to find element: %@", error);
  return noErr;
}
[element setStringValue:[metadata valueForKey:(id)kMDItemDisplayName]];

//Updating the description
error = nil;
element = [[template nodesForXPath:@"/html/body/div/*[@id='description']"
                       error:&error] lastObject];
if (!element) {
  NSLog(@"Failed to find element: %@", error);
  return noErr;
}
[element setStringValue:[metadata valueForKey:(id)kMDItemTextContent]];

//Updating the serves value
error = nil;
element = [[template nodesForXPath:@"/html/body/div/*[@id='serves']"
                       error:&error] lastObject];
if (!element) {
  NSLog(@"Failed to find element: %@", error);
  return noErr;
}
NSNumber *serves = [metadata valueForKey:@"kPPServes"];
[element setStringValue:[NSString stringWithFormat:@"Serves: %i",
                        [serves integerValue]]];

//Updating the last served value
error = nil;
element = [[template nodesForXPath:@"/html/body/div/*[@id='last_served']"
                       error:&error] lastObject];
if (!element) {
  NSLog(@"Failed to find element: %@", error);
  return noErr;
}
NSDate *lastServedDate = [metadata valueForKey:(id)kMDItemLastUsedDate];
if (lastServedDate) {
  NSDateFormatter *dateFormatter;
  dateFormatter = [[[NSDateFormatter alloc] init]  autorelease];
  [dateFormatter setDateStyle:NSDateFormatterMediumStyle];
  [dateFormatter setTimeStyle:NSDateFormatterNoStyle];
  [element setStringValue:[NSString stringWithFormat:@"Last Served: %@",
                          [dateFormatter stringFromDate:lastServedDate]]];
} else {
  [element setStringValue:@"Last Served: Never"];
}
```

Since we know the shape of the HTML document, we can build simple
XPath queries to retrieve each part of the document and replace its
value component with data from our metadata in NSDictionary.

Spotlight/QuickLookPlugin/GeneratePreviewForURL.m

```
    QLPreviewRequestSetDataRepresentation(preview,
                                    (CFDataRef)[template XMLData],
                                    kUTTypeHTML,
                                    (CFDictionaryRef)properties);
  } @finally {
    [pool release], pool = nil;
  }
  return noErr;
}
```

Once all the data has been put into the HTML document, it is time to render it and set the QLPreviewRequestRef. As you can see in this section of code, we are passing in the reference along with the HTML file as data and the properties NSDictionary. When this is complete, we pop the NSAutoreleasePool and return noErr. Quick Look will now generate our preview and present it to the user.

Testing the Quick Look Plug-In

At the time of this writing, testing the Quick Look plug-in is a bit more challenging than its Spotlight counterpart. Although there is still a command-line option to test it, getting the system to recognize the plug-in is a bit trickier. The issue is that the system tends to ignore what generator you want it to use and will use the generator defined for the system.

In writing this chapter, I used the following workflow to test the Quick Look plug-in:

1. Clean and build the main recipe application.

2. On the command line, execute qlmanage -r to reset the Quick Look generators.

3. Run the recipe application, which causes our Quick Look generator to get registered.

4. From the command line (can also be done inside of Xcode), I ran qlmanage -p ${path to metadata test file}, which generated the preview. Using the -t switch instead would produce the thumbnail.

5. Rinse and repeat.

I hope by the time you read this the workflow will have improved. There is a -g switch available on the qlmanage command line that should

Figure 7.8: DISPLAYING THE METADATA FILES IN A SMART FOLDER

override the system generator, but unfortunately it does not appear to work at this time.

7.3 Putting It All Together

With a Spotlight importer and a Quick Look generator, it is possible to do some very interesting things in Mac OS X. For example, we can build a smart folder that finds all our recipes. We can then put that smart folder in the sidebar of Finder and be able to easily access all our recipes directly from the Finder. Further, we can turn on Cover Flow for this smart folder and smoothly browse through the pictures of our recipes. See Figure 7.8.

With the included metadata, this opens up quite a few ideas. For example, along with each recipe, we are storing the time it was last served in the metadata. We can use this information to further refine our smart folder to display only those recipes that we have not served in the last thirty days. It is possible to get quite creative with metadata now that the operating system is aware of it.

7.4 Taking It Further

Further Use of UTIs

With UTIs it is possible to integrate even further with the operating system, Spotlight, and Quick Look. It is possible to publish a full description of the UTI—effectively injecting it into the tree and thus having the data type appear in Spotlight rules and more. However, this is beyond the scope of this book.

Decreasing the Size of the Metadata Files

This is probably very similar to how Core Data does it internally in Snow Leopard.

Depending on the application, it is possible to reduce the metadata files dramatically. Since the importer (and the generator) can stand up the entire Core Data stack, it is possible to just have the NSManaged-ObjectID (or even a unique identifier within the Recipe object) stored in the metadata file and have the importers and generators retrieve all the metadata information from the Core Data stack instead. This would also simplify the updating of the metadata since the only action required at that point would be to delete metadata files for records that no longer exist. However, care must be taken with this approach because performance may suffer greatly.

Improving the Quick Look Thumbnail Generator

You may have noticed that we ignored the max size setting of the Quick Look thumbnail generator. That was done for the sake of clarity, and in a production system we should be sizing down the image to accommodate that setting. By doing so, we would be good citizens as well as be helping the performance of Quick Look whenever our files are involved.

Document-Based Applications

When writing an application that uses a document model as opposed to a single repository, then integrating Spotlight and Quick Look is even easier. Instead of having separate metadata files, we can simply store the relevant information in the metadata of the actual documents. This allows the importers to read the metadata without having to initialize the entire Core Data stack and still allows for very quick access to the relevant information.

Chapter 8

Sync Services and Core Data

Cloud computing is in our future. Users do not want to have to worry about which computer they stored their data on. It brings great peace of mind to me knowing that when I enter a new contact on my laptop while I am out, it will get synced to my other computers and my phone. For every application where it makes sense to share data across computers, it is incumbent upon us as developers to make the option available to our users.

Fortunately, Apple has made huge advances in Sync Services in Leopard. One of those improvements was to integrate Sync Services with Core Data. Although it is still nontrivial to utilize Sync Services, it is significantly simpler than it was in Tiger, and when combined with Core Data, it is even easier than it would be without that combination.

When our data is stored in Core Data and we are writing an application that is at least Leopard targeted, Sync Services can use the Core Data model directly to get information about the data to be synced. In addition, since the data format of Core Data is known as far as the Sync Services APIs are concerned, the amount of code required to perform a sync is one line. For anyone who has written Sync Services code under a previous version of Mac OS X, this will be a welcome change.

Although the sync operation itself is only one line of code, quite a bit of work is still required to get syncing working correctly. We will need to configure our data model properly for Sync Services, create a sync schema, and add the syncing logic to our application, and we will need to make a couple of changes to our persistent store coordinator.

Overall, adding syncing to an application can be quite a challenge, but the end result is definitely worth it. When we are done, our users will not have to worry about which Mac they added or updated their recipe on. Simply updating the recipe on their laptop will cause it to get updated on every other Mac they have.

8.1 Sync Services Fundamentals

Conceptually, Sync Services works on the principle of a single source of truth. That truth is stored at the operating system level and operates very much like a database. Each entity for each application is stored in the truth as a single record, and the truth keeps track of every change to every entity.

Sync Clients

Every application, device, server, or peer[1] is considered a client to Sync Services and talks to the truth. Even if an application is the source of that data, like our recipes application is, it is still considered a client of the truth, and therefore it syncs to that truth.

As a client, it is expected that our application will register with the truth and give it a description. That description will let the truth know our name, the image to use when talking about us, and what entities we care about. The entities part is what makes Sync Services very powerful. We can subscribe to more data than we produce. For instance, we could receive sync notifications for calendars, contacts, or bookmarks if we were interested. Although we will be paying attention to only our recipe objects at this time, it is definitely *possible* to listen for more.

As part of the registration, each client defines a callback method that Sync Services will use to let the client know that a sync is about to happen. The client can choose not to participate in the sync at that time, but generally, it is a good idea to be part of the sync. Sync Services will not call a client unless data it cares about is being synced.

When a sync is performed, there are three steps to the sync process: push, mingle, and pull. During the push phase, each client pushes all changes it has that have occurred since the last sync. Once the truth has received all the changes from all the clients, a mingle is performed. The mingle merges all the changes from all the clients into a single data set. This mingle happens entirely within the truth, and clients simply wait for this phase to be over. Once the mingle phase is complete, the

---

1. Currently the only server available is MobileMe, and there are no provisions for peers.

pull phase occurs. In the pull phase, each client pulls down the changes from the truth and updates their internal data stores to match. When the pull phase is complete, then the sync is finished.

Sync Schemas

A sync schema has a lot of similarities to a database schema. Each sync schema describes how data is structured for one or more data classes. These data classes are not objects but are types of data. For instance, contacts is *one* class of data. Calendar data is also *one* class of data. Our recipes will also be *one* class of data. It is possible to have more than one data class in a schema, but for our application we will have only one.

In addition to describing the data class, the sync schema will also define all the entities that are part of that data class. For our application, each of the entities that is in our data model will also be in our sync schema. For each entity, all of its attributes and its relationships are described. For each of those, all of the details are made available. For instance, an attribute would be described as required, string, and so on. For a relationship, it would describe what it is a relationship to, whether it is one-to-one, one-to-many, and so on.

Finally, a sync schema contains the name of the schema and an image associated with the schema that Sync Services can use when asking for user input. If we look at the Sync tab of MobileMe in the system preferences, we can see an example of this interaction, as shown in Figure 8.1, on the following page.

Don't Panic!

I am sure, after reading all of this, that the thought of adding Sync Services to your application is absolutely terrifying. I know that when I did it the first time, it certainly was. However, there is a light at the end of the tunnel for those of us who are fortunate enough to be using Core Data. With Leopard, most of this has already been done for us!

Since Core Data represents a *known* data structure, the engineers within Apple were kind enough to do all of the heavy lifting for us to integrate Sync Services into our applications. All that is required of us is to link everything together.

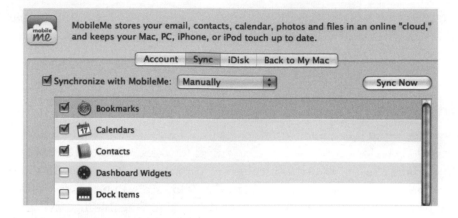

Figure 8.1: MOBILEME SYSTEM PREFERENCES

8.2 Updating Our Data Model

The first step in making our application ready for Sync Services is to update the data model to reflect what we want synced, what is considered an identity item (similar in concept to a primary key in database terms), and what triggers a "data changed" notification. All of this is configured directly with the data model, and fortunately making these changes does not trigger a version difference in the data model itself, so we do not have to create new data and mapping models.

Setting the Data Class

One of the confusing things about Sync Services is some of the terminology that is used. One example of that is the data class. Coming from Core Data, one would think this refers to an object class that describes the data. That, unfortunately, is not its meaning with Sync Services. Instead, it is a unique identifier that defines a logical grouping of data. For instance, the entire Address Book's data model is called the com.apple.contacts data class. For our application, our data class will be com.pragprog.GrokkingRecipes. This is the value that we will assign to every entity in the data model. You will note that when we enter this value, Xcode automatically appends the name of the entity itself to the end of the data class's name. This creates a unique name for each entity.

Attribute and Relationship Names

Each attribute and relationship within each entity also has its own unique name. The format for the attributes and relationships is DataClass.EntityName/AttributeName. For example, the name of the recipe entity would be referred to as com.pragprog.GrokkingRecipes.Recipe/name.

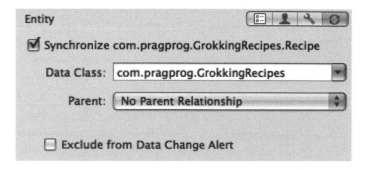

Figure 8.2: SETTING THE DATA CLASS

Setting the Identity Properties

Once the data class has been set for each entity in the data model, the next step is to set which attributes and/or relationships are identity properties for the sake of Sync Services. The purpose of this setting is to tell Sync Services which attributes or relationships it should use to match up records between applications, servers, or peers. When Sync Services attempts to merge data from two different sources, it looks to these identity properties to find records that would be considered the same. For example, if we were merging recipe data from two computers via MobileMe and we were looking at the Author entities, we would compare the name attribute of each author. If the name is the same, then we would consider it to be the same record for syncing purposes.

Author Settings

For the author, the settings are very simple since the object itself is very simple. We set the name attribute to be the identity property, and neither the name nor the recipes is excluded from the data change alerts.

Ingredient Settings

The ingredient entity is configured virtually identically to the Author entity. The name attribute will still be used as the identity property; all the rest of the attributes and relationships will be included for syncing, and none of them is excluded from data change alerts.

Recipe Settings

The Recipe entity has a special situation. First, the imagePath is very specific to the machine that the recipe is being stored on. It is unlikely (and unnecessary) that this path will be the same on more than one machine. Therefore, we will not be syncing this attribute. However, we do want the image itself to be synced across the machines. To accomplish this, we will change the entity slightly; we'll add a new attribute called image and configure it as optional and transient. By flagging it as transient, we will not have to worry about a version change for the data model. As you will recall, setting it as transient will also mean that it is not stored in our repository, which is exactly what we want. Although we do not want it stored in the repository, we do want to sync it across machines. Therefore, we will make sure that the Synchronize option is set to YES. To complete this attribute, we need to add logic to our PPRecipe object to handle the image.

SyncServices/PPRecipe.m

```
- (NSData*)image
{
  NSLog(@"%@:%s entered", [self class], _cmd);
  if (image) return image;
  NSString *path = [self primitiveValueForKey:@"imagePath"];
  if (!path) return nil;
  image = [[NSData alloc] initWithContentsOfFile:path];
  return image;
}


- (void)setImage:(NSData*)data
{
  NSLog(@"%@:%s entered", [self class], _cmd);
  NSString *destPath = [self primitiveValueForKey:@"imagePath"];
  if (!destPath) {
    //Build the path we want the file to be at
    destPath = [[NSApp delegate] applicationSupportFolder];
    NSString *guid = [[NSProcessInfo processInfo] globallyUniqueString];
    destPath = [destPath stringByAppendingPathComponent:guid];
    [self setValue:destPath forKey:@"imagePath"];
  }
  [data writeToFile:destPath atomically:NO];
```

```
  [data retain];
  [image release];
  image = data;
}
```

In the accessor methods that we added to the PPRecipe object, we are retrieving the image data that is stored on the disk at imagePath. When the data is being set and the imagePath is not set, then we will create a new file in our Application Support directory and save it. These accessors now allow for the image to be passed around for Sync Services without it being stored in the repository.

As for the rest of the attributes and relationships, they are all flagged to be synced, and only the name attribute is flagged to be an identity property.

RecipeIngredient Settings

The RecipeIngredient entity is an unusual one to sync. Since it is basically a join table (to borrow from database terminology), there is no attribute that identifies it as unique. Therefore, we will sync its one attribute, quantity, but we will flag its relationships as the identity properties. By flagging all three relationships as the identity of the record, we are guaranteed uniqueness for each combination of Ingredient, Recipe, and UnitOfMeasure.

Type Settings

For the Type entity, we are syncing this object only to preserve the relationships across sync clients. Although this data will never change and therefore does not really need to be synced, we do want to sync the relationships between Type entities and Recipe entities. Therefore, we flag the name as the identity property and include its relationships in the sync.

UnitOfMeasure

Like the Author entity, this entity has the name attribute as its identity property and has its relationships included in the sync.

8.3 Creating the Sync Schema

Now that our data model is ready for syncing, it is time to build the sync schema itself. The sync schema is used by Mac OS X to describe our interaction with and integration into the syncing ecosystem. If we were not using Core Data, we would be describing every entity, attribute, and relationship inside of the sync schema. Fortunately, since we are using Core Data, that part is not necessary. What this leaves to be included in the schema is to define the data classes, the localization, and the icon to be used by Sync Services whenever it is talking about our data class. When we are done, we will have another bundle to be included in our application that we will reference when dealing with Sync Services.

Setting Up the Sync Schema Subproject

Just like the Spotlight and Quick Look subprojects that we created in Chapter 7, *Spotlight, Quick Look, and Core Data*, on page 109, we will add a third subproject to our recipes application. Just like the previous two, the sync schema project template is under the Standard Apple Plugins section in Xcode. Once the subproject is created, we drag the project into our main project and define it as a dependency in the application target. Once the dependency is set up, then add the .syncschema bundle to the Copy Bundle Resources phase of the target.

Creating the Schema.plist

Although it is possible to add custom code to a sync schema to help display the data when the sync error dialog box is displayed, for our purposes we really need to set up only the Schema.plist file. The header and implementation files that are created with the template can be removed because we will not be needing them.

The Schema.plist file describes everything that Sync Services needs to know about our data. For our needs, we need to set three keys within this plist: DataClasses, ManagedObjectModels, and Name.

DataClasses Key

The DataClasses key has two values, a Name and an ImagePath. The Name value is meant to be localized and therefore does not need to be user friendly in this file. For our recipes, I named the data class com.pragprog.GrokkingRecipes. The only requirement is that this name be unique. Therefore, a reverse dot notation will help to guarantee that. The other value, ImagePath, needs to point to an image file that Sync Services will use whenever it is referring to our data. For example, this image is used in the system preferences and in the data change alert dialog boxes. For our needs, the application icon is sufficient for this, so we include a copy of it within the sync schema bundle.

ManagedObjectModels Key

The ManagedObjectModels key is an array of file references pointing to .mom files. Note that this key will not accept versioned managed object model bundles, and therefore we need to point to a specific version of our model. Since we are currently on version 3 of the model, we will point this to that model. This key can accept more than one model, so if we had split up our data model into multiple managed object model files, we would add all of them here.

Name Key

This name attribute refers to the name of the *schema* as opposed to the name of the data. This name is used internally in Sync Services and is not exposed to the user at all. Since we have only one data class in our application, we can name the schema the same as the data class, com.pragprog.GrokkingRecipes.

Localizing Schema.strings

Although our application is not localized for any language other than English, we need to create a strings file for the sync schema. This localization file will translate the unique identifiers into human-readable names when Sync Services displays information about our data. Just like other localization files, this file is a list of name-value pairs with the unique names of our data class, entities, attributes, and relationships as the name half and the human-readable counterpart as the value.

```
/* Localized strings for GrokkingRecipes */

"com.pragprog.GrokkingRecipes" = "Grokking Recipes";

"com.pragprog.GrokkingRecipes.Author" = "Author Entity";
"com.pragprog.GrokkingRecipes.Author/name" = "Author Name";

"com.pragprog.GrokkingRecipes.Ingredient" = "Ingredient Entity";
"com.pragprog.GrokkingRecipes.Ingredient/cost" = "Cost";
"com.pragprog.GrokkingRecipes.Ingredient/name" = "Ingredient Name";
"com.pragprog.GrokkingRecipes.Ingredient/quantity" = "Quantity";

"com.pragprog.GrokkingRecipes.Recipe" = "Recipe Entity";
"com.pragprog.GrokkingRecipes.Recipe/type" = "Recipe Type";
"com.pragprog.GrokkingRecipes.Recipe/desc" = "Description";
"com.pragprog.GrokkingRecipes.Recipe/lastUsed" = "Last Used";
"com.pragprog.GrokkingRecipes.Recipe/name" = "Recipe Name";
"com.pragprog.GrokkingRecipes.Recipe/serves" = "Serves";

"com.pragprog.GrokkingRecipes.RecipeIngredient" = "Quantity Entity";
"com.pragprog.GrokkingRecipes.RecipeIngredient/quantity" = "Quantity";
```

```
"com.pragprog.GrokkingRecipes.Type" = "Type Entity";
"com.pragprog.GrokkingRecipes.Type/name" = "Name";

"com.pragprog.GrokkingRecipes.UnitOfMeasure" = "Unit of Measure Entity";
"com.pragprog.GrokkingRecipes.UnitOfMeasure/name" = "Name";
```

8.4 Creating the Client Description File

Now that we have our schema put together, it is time to build the client description file. This file is different from the sync schema we just built because it is coming at the sync from the client's point of view. The sync schema tells Sync Services what data will be synced, and the client description tells Sync Services what data *this application* will be syncing. It is quite possible to have a client that wants only a subset of the data and does not care about certain parts. For example, if we wanted to build a dashboard widget that displayed recipes, it may not care about the author and therefore would not add it to its client description.

Since we are the primary application for this schema, we will sync all the data available. This file is called ClientDescription.plist, and it is part of the primary application bundle and will be included in the Resources subdirectory of the application bundle. Inside of this plist are four keys: DisplayName, ImagePath, Type, and Entities. DisplayName and ImagePath are both used when Sync Services needs to display specific information about this client as opposed to information about the schema itself. However, since our application is the primary application for this schema (as opposed to calendar or contact data), we can use the same name and image that we used for the schema. The Type key defines what type of client we are, with options of app, device, server, or peer. For our application, that answer is app.

This leaves the Entities key. The Entities key tells Sync Services which entities our client cares about and the attributes/relationships of those entities. Since we are the primary application, we care about all the entities, their attributes, and the relationships.

SyncServices/ClientDescription.plist

```
<?xml version="1.0" encoding="UTF-8"?>
<!DOCTYPE plist PUBLIC "-//Apple//DTD PLIST 1.0//EN"
  "http://www.apple.com/DTDs/PropertyList-1.0.dtd">
<plist version="1.0">
<dict>
  <key>DisplayName</key>
```

```xml
<string>Grokking Recipes</string>
<key>ImagePath</key>
<string>App.icns</string>
<key>Type</key>
<string>app</string>
<key>Entities</key>
<dict>
  <key>com.pragprog.GrokkingRecipes.Author</key>
  <array>
    <string>com.apple.syncservices.RecordEntityName</string>
    <string>name</string>
    <string>recipes</string>
  </array>
  <key>com.pragprog.GrokkingRecipes.Ingredient</key>
  <array>
    <string>com.apple.syncservices.RecordEntityName</string>
    <string>cost</string>
    <string>name</string>
    <string>quantity</string>
    <string>recipes</string>
    <string>unitOfMeasure</string>
  </array>
  <key>com.pragprog.GrokkingRecipes.Recipe</key>
  <array>
    <string>com.apple.syncservices.RecordEntityName</string>
    <string>desc</string>
    <string>lastUsed</string>
    <string>name</string>
    <string>serves</string>
    <string>type</string>
    <string>author</string>
    <string>ingredients</string>
    <string>image</string>
  </array>
  <key>com.pragprog.GrokkingRecipes.RecipeIngredient</key>
  <array>
    <string>com.apple.syncservices.RecordEntityName</string>
    <string>quantity</string>
    <string>unitOfMeasure</string>
    <string>ingredient</string>
    <string>recipe</string>
  </array>
  <key>com.pragprog.GrokkingRecipes.Type</key>
  <array>
    <string>com.apple.syncservices.RecordEntityName</string>
    <string>name</string>
  </array>
  <key>com.pragprog.GrokkingRecipes.UnitOfMeasure</key>
  <array>
    <string>com.apple.syncservices.RecordEntityName</string>
    <string>name</string>
```

```
        <string>ingredients</string>
        <string>recipeIngredients</string>
      </array>
    </dict>
  </dict>
</plist>
```

8.5 Modifying the NSPersistentStoreCoordinator

One thing that always has to be remembered about Sync Services is that we want it to be fast—the faster, the better. If it gets slowed down, then all kinds of bad things can happen. For instance, the computer can go to sleep in the middle of the sync, the user can quit the application, network connections can go down—the list goes on. Therefore, we want to make sure that when a sync actually happens, it happens very quickly. Unfortunately, Core Data, although being a fast process in its own environment, can be too slow for syncing purposes. To address this, the NSPersistentStoreCoordinator has an additional method included in a category as part of the Sync Services framework. This method, set-StoresFastSyncDetailsAtURL:forPersistentStore:, defines an additional store to be used by Sync Services to store information in preparation for the next sync operation. This additional store is not a copy of the data but has similarities to notes about the various objects in our NSPersistentStore that can be used during the sync process to speed things up.

It should be noted that without this additional setting, syncing of a Core Data repository will not work. If you run into an issue with another application and syncing is not working, be sure to check that the fast sync store is being set and created.

Adding this store to our application requires a small change to our -persistentStoreCoordinator method.

SyncServices/AppDelegate.m

```
NSPersistentStore *store;
store = [persistentStoreCoordinator addPersistentStoreWithType:NSXMLStoreType
                                                 configuration:nil
                                                           URL:url
                                                       options:nil
                                                         error:&error];

if (!store) {
  NSLog(@"%@:%s presenting error no store", [self class], _cmd);
  [[NSApplication sharedApplication] presentError:error];
  return nil;
}
```

```
NSString *fss = @"GrokkingRecipes.fastsyncstore";
fss = [applicationSupportFolder stringByAppendingPathComponent:fss];
NSURL *fsdURL = [NSURL fileURLWithPath:fss];

[persistentStoreCoordinator setStoresFastSyncDetailsAtURL:fsdURL
                                      forPersistentStore:store];

return persistentStoreCoordinator;
```

In this code snippet there are two important changes. First, instead of checking to see whether the call to addPersistentStoreWithType:configuration:URL:options:error: returned a nil or not, we assign its result to a local variable. We do this so that we can pass it into the setStoresFastSyncDetailsAtURL:forPersistentStore: method further down. Next we build a path for the fast sync store to be written to. Since we are storing our data in the Application Support folder, it makes sense to just store it alongside the primary persistent store. If we were using a document application, then it might make sense to store it somewhere else or with a unique filename. Once the path is built, we pass that path along with our reference to the NSPersistentStore to the category method setStoresFastSyncDetailsAtURL:forPersistentStore: on our NSPersistentStoreCoordinator. That is the only change we need to make to our Core Data stack to enable Sync Services support.

8.6 Creating the Sync Helper

Now it is time to put all the pieces together. Although this piece can be put just about anywhere, I decided to separate all the sync code into its own class for clarity. When I originally wrote this code, I had put it into the AppDelegate.m but quickly decided that it was causing that object to be too complex and hard to follow. Therefore, I decided to separate the syncing code into a small helper class.

NSPersistentStoreCoordinatorSyncing

As I mentioned in the fundamentals (Section 8.1, *Sync Services Fundamentals*, on page 136), Sync Services needs a callback to let our client know what is going on. To be completely accurate, we need both a callback and a protocol. The callback is used by Sync Services to let our application know that a sync is about to happen. The protocol allows us to listen in to that sync and answer questions as things go by. Our sync helper will implement that protocol named NSPersistentStoreCoordinatorSyncing.

Every method within this protocol is considered optional, but there are two that I think should be considered required. Although I have implemented all the methods in the example project, it is the following two methods that are most important:

- -managedObjectContextsToMonitorWhenSyncingPersistentStoreCoordinator:. This method, in our application, returns our single NSManagedObjectContext. The purpose of this method is to tell Sync Services which contexts to monitor during the sync just in case our user gets clever (and quick!) and alters the data during a sync. Without implementing this method, it is quite possible to get conflicts between the truth and our internal NSManagedObjectContext.

- -managedObjectContextsToReloadAfterSyncingPersistentStoreCoordinator:. This is similar to the previous method mentioned; our implementation of this method simply returns our single NSManagedObjectContext. Also, like the previous method, I consider this one required because we want our context reloaded after the sync has completed so that our user can see the updated information. I can certainly imagine situations where we would not want this, but for our application, none of those situations applies.

The rest of the methods in the protocol allow us to be notified when a sync has finished and tell us what is being pushed, pulled, and canceled. By using the rest of this protocol, we can provide feedback to the user, inject special case changes to the sync itself, or just monitor its progress. Although I have implemented these methods in the example code, they are optional and can be removed for brevity.

Registering as a Sync Client

When our application starts up and after we have checked our metadata per Chapter 7, *Spotlight, Quick Look, and Core Data*, we want to register our application as a sync client. Since all the sync-handling code is contained within SyncHelper, the only thing we need to do here is initialize an instance of it.

`SyncServices/AppDelegate.m`

```
NSError *error = nil;
syncHelper = [[SyncHelper alloc] initWithDelegate:self error:&error];
if (!syncHelper) {
  NSLog(@"%@:%s presenting error sync helper failed", [self class], _cmd);
  NSDictionary *ui = [error userInfo];
```

```
  for (NSError *suberror in [ui valueForKey:NSDetailedErrorsKey]) {
    NSLog(@"subError: %@", suberror);
  }
  [NSApp presentError:error];
}
error = nil;
```

Our SyncHelper takes two parameters on initialization: a reference to
our AppDelegate and a pointer to an NSError. If something goes wrong in
the registration, the NSError will get populated, and the SyncHelper will
return nil. If that occurs, then we will present the error to the user and
continue.

Inside the SyncHelper, we assign the reference to the AppDelegate to an
ivar and attempt to register ourselves as a client to Sync Services and
start a sync.

`SyncServices/SyncHelper.m`

```
- (id)initWithDelegate:(id)_delegate error:(NSError**)error
{
  if (!(self = [super init])) return nil;
  delegate = _delegate;

  ISyncClient *client = [self syncClient:error];
  if (!client) {
    [self autorelease];
    return nil;
  }
  [client setSyncAlertHandler:self
                     selector:@selector(client:mightWantToSyncEntityNames:)];
  if (![self performSync:error]) {
    [self autorelease];
    return nil;
  }

  return self;
}
```

In this method, we set this instance of the SyncHelper to be the callback for Sync Services to notify when a sync is about to start external to our application. When that occurs, we will receive a message to
-client:mightWantToSyncEntityNames:, and we can react accordingly. The
most complex part of this object initialization is getting a reference
to the ISyncClient object. Since getting this reference will occur several
times within the life cycle of our application, it has been put into its
own method.

SyncServices/SyncHelper.m

```
- (ISyncClient*)syncClient:(NSError**)error
{
  NSString *ident = [[NSBundle mainBundle] bundleIdentifier];
  ISyncClient *client;
  NSDictionary *dict;
  ISyncManager *manager = [ISyncManager sharedManager];
  NSBundle *mainBundle = [NSBundle mainBundle];

  @try {
    client = [manager clientWithIdentifier:ident];
    if (client) return client;
```

The first thing that we do when trying to get a reference to our ISyncClient is to request it from the ISyncManager using our bundle identifier as our name. If we have previously registered with the ISyncManager, then this will return our client, and we are done. If this is our first time through this process, then that call will return a nil, and we will have to register with the ISyncManager.

SyncServices/SyncHelper.m

```
NSString *path = [mainBundle pathForResource:@"GrokkingRecipes"
                                      ofType:@"syncschema"];
if (![manager registerSchemaWithBundlePath:path]) {
  NSString *err = NSLocalizedString(@"Failed to register the schema",
    @"Failed to register the schema error message");
  dict = [NSDictionary dictionaryWithObject:err
                                     forKey:NSLocalizedDescriptionKey];
  *error = [NSError errorWithDomain:@"PragProg"
                               code:8001
                           userInfo:dict];
  return nil;
}
```

This is where the sync schema that we built comes into play. Since our client has not been registered, then we know, since we are the originator of the data, that our schema has also not been registered. Therefore, the first step is to find the GrokkingRecipes.syncschema bundle within our application and register it with the ISyncManager. If this is not successful, then we populate the NSError and return nil. Assuming that it is successful, the next step is to register our client.

SyncServices/SyncHelper.m

```
path = [mainBundle pathForResource:@"ClientDescription"
                            ofType:@"plist"];
client = [manager registerClientWithIdentifier:ident
                            descriptionFilePath:path];
```

With the schema registered, we need to now register our client. Here we grab a reference to the ClientDescription.plist that we created previously and pass it to the ISyncManager along with our unique identifier. This will register our client and return a reference to our ISyncClient object. Now that our client is registered, we need to turn on syncing with all of the other client types. This allows us to decide which syncs we want to be involved in. Again, since we are the originator of the data, we want to be involved in every sync.

SyncServices/SyncHelper.m

```
[client setShouldSynchronize:YES
         withClientsOfType:ISyncClientTypeApplication];
[client setShouldSynchronize:YES
         withClientsOfType:ISyncClientTypeDevice];
[client setShouldSynchronize:YES
         withClientsOfType:ISyncClientTypeServer];
[client setShouldSynchronize:YES
         withClientsOfType:ISyncClientTypePeer];
```

The last step in this method is to capture and handle any exceptions that we receive. As of the writing of this book, there are still a few exceptions that this process can throw, so we want to be sure to capture those, wrap them up in an NSError,[2] and hand the back to our caller. Assuming nothing has blown up on us, we return the ISyncClient.

SyncServices/SyncHelper.m

```
  } @catch (NSException *exception) {
    dict = [NSDictionary dictionaryWithObject:[exception reason]
                                    forKey:NSLocalizedDescriptionKey];
    *error = [NSError errorWithDomain:@"PragProg"
                          code:8002
                       userInfo:dict];
    return nil;
  }
  return client;
}
```

Performing a Sync

Now that we have registered our schema and our sync client, we need to be able to handle the two ways a sync can occur. We can either initiate the sync or receive a notification that a sync is about to occur. Fortunately, we handle both of these situations in the same manner.

---

2. Where they belong anyway.

When a sync is about to start, the first thing we want to do is perform a save on our NSManagedObjectContext. Once that is completed, then we can tell Sync Services that we are ready to perform a sync. Therefore, we need to make a small alteration to our global save method. Since we already put all our save logic in one method in Chapter 7, *Spotlight, Quick Look, and Core Data*, on page 109, it makes perfect sense to kick off our sync operations from there.

SyncServices/AppDelegate.m

```
NSLog(@"%@:%s Performing sync", [self class], _cmd);
if (![syncHelper performSync:error]) {
  return NO;
}
```

As soon as the save operation returns, we want to call our SyncHelper and ask it to -performSync:. We pass in an NSError into this method so that we can be notified if an error occurred during the sync.

SyncServices/SyncHelper.m

```
- (BOOL)performSync:(NSError**)err;
{
  ISyncClient *client = [self syncClient:err];
  if (!client) return NO;

  NSLog(@"Starting sync");
  NSPersistentStoreCoordinator *store = [delegate persistentStoreCoordinator];
  return [store syncWithClient:client
                  inBackground:YES
                       handler:self
                         error:err];
}
```

In the -performSync: method, we grab a fresh reference to our ISyncClient and a reference to our NSPersistentStoreCoordinator. With both of those, we will use the second method added to the NSPersistentStoreCoordinator in the Sync Services category and request a sync via the syncWithClient:inBackground:handler:error: method. If there is a failure in the sync, then a NO will be returned to the caller, and the NSError will be populated. Since we are passing the SyncHelper as the handler for this sync, it will receive all of the notifications discussed earlier because of it implementing the NSPersistentStoreCoordinatorSyncing protocol.

To make sure that our metadata is up-to-date, we want to flesh out one of the delegate callback methods, specifically, -persistentStoreCoordinator:didFinishSyncSession:. In this method, we want to check to see whether our

NSManagedObjectContext has any changes in it and, if it does, update the metadata and save the context.

The last thing we need to do is handle an external sync request. Since we already defined -client:mightWantToSyncEntityNames: as the method to be called when an external sync starts, we need to request a save at that point.

SyncServices/SyncHelper.m

```
- (void)client:(ISyncClient*)client mightWantToSyncEntityNames:(NSArray*)names
{
  NSError *error = nil;
  if (![delegate save:&error]) {
    [NSApp presentError:error];
  }
}
```

Since our call to save the NSManagedObjectContext will also kick off a sync, there is nothing more that we need to do.

8.7 The Syncrospector

Sync Services has the added complexity of being rather difficult to debug and test. Since the truth is effectively a black box, normally all we can do is poke at it and watch the responses. Fortunately, in the more recent builds of Xcode, Apple has given us a working copy of a development tool called Syncrospector. You can locate the Syncrospector in the Developer directory (wherever you decided to install it, normally at /Developer), in the Applications folder, and finally in the Utilities subfolder. This tool allows us to peek inside the truth and even reset data or force different types of syncs.

Clients Pane

The Clients pane shows all the known clients of Sync Services. Within this pane we can see whether our client is registered properly, what data classes it has registered, and the state of each entity. We can also force a sync of the client from this pane. See Figure 8.3, on the following page. Of all the panes available inside the Syncrospector, this is one of the two that I use most often.

Truth Pane

The Truth pane allows us to look at the data that is currently in the truth. We can see, for each entity, when it was last updated and who

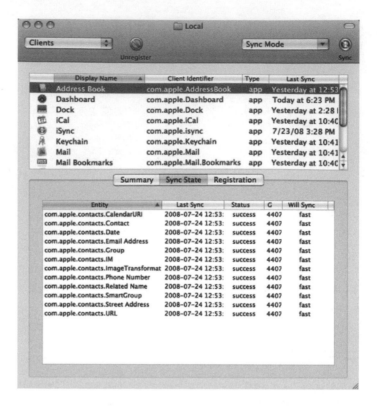

Figure 8.3: SYNCROSPECTOR CLIENTS PANE

changed it. I find this pane to be useful when trying to figure out what went wrong with my data and to see who mucked it up.

History Pane

The History pane allows us to see every transaction that has ever occurred inside the truth. With this pane, it is possible to track down where data got mangled and by whom, no matter how long ago it occurred.

Schema Pane

The Schema pane is the other that I use very frequently. It shows all the schemas that are registered within the truth and allows us to inspect all their details. In addition, it is possible to delete a schema from the truth via this pane. Finally, this pane is useful for clearing data from the truth and clients. This is very helpful during testing.

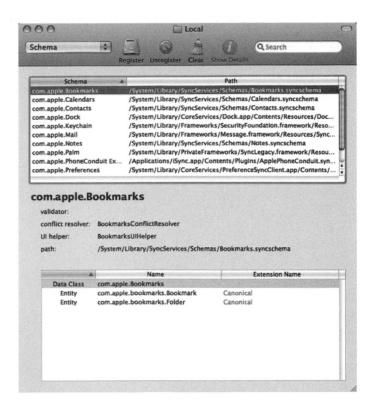

Figure 8.4: SYNCROSPECTOR SCHEMA PANE

8.8 Wrapping Up

Since this book is focused on Core Data, we haven't covered quite a few areas of Sync Services. For a true breadth of knowledge on this framework, you should research the following subjects in more depth.

Schema Versioning

This subject is currently in flux and may change by the time you read this book. As it stands today, if your schema needs to change, then ideally all your clients of that data should get updated to the latest schema. If they don't, then your users may get inconsistent results.

In addition, schemas are tied to a particular version of the NSManaged-ObjectModel. Therefore, if the data model changes, then chances are a new schema will be needed, or at least it will need to reference the latest data model.

Syncing with Devices, Servers, and Peers

This chapter covers syncing with the truth. The truth can also sync with MobileMe (currently one of the most useful features of Sync Services), devices, and peers. Although there are no peers defined at this time, it does not mean there never will be. In addition, it is quite common to sync with devices, and I suspect that Sync Services will become available for the iPhone at some time in the near future.

Chapter 9

Multithreading and Core Data

Chances are your primary machine has at least two cores in it. I also would not be surprised if every machine you develop on has at least two cores or even more. Multithreading is soon going to be necessary for every moderately complex application that runs on Mac OS X. This is something that we as developers need to accept and plan for while developing our applications. Fortunately, there are new features in Mac OS X that make multithreading easier for us and less error prone

The problem, however, is that Core Data is not inherently thread safe. It still wants and expects to be run in a single thread. Therefore, when we start multithreading our applications, we must take care to work with Core Data properly to avoid threading issues.

9.1 Why Isn't Core Data Thread Safe?

You may be surprised to learn that there are a lot of things in Cocoa and Objective-C that are not thread safe and that Core Data is only one of many. For instance, whenever you make a change to a GUI widget, it is recommended that you be on the main thread because the UI is not thread safe.

The biggest issue with dealing with Core Data in multiple threads is keeping the NSManagedObjectContext in sync. When a change is made to an NSManagedObject on a thread that is different from the one that created the NSManagedObjectContext, the context is not aware of it and can have potentially stale data. This is the part of Core Data that is not thread safe. The NSPersistentStore, NSPersistentStoreCoordinator, and NSManagedObjectModel are all perfectly thread safe, but the NSManagedObjectContext is not.

> ### NSOperation and NSOperationQueue
>
> Throughout this chapter we will be using NSOperation and NSOperationQueue quite heavily. These are classes that were added to Cocoa as part of Mac OS X 10.5 Leopard specifically to make threading easier. Although we will not be going into detail on how to use these classes, it is of extreme value to fully learn these classes so that you can use them properly in your own projects.
>
> Often one naming issue causes some confusion while using NSOperation. The NSOperation uses a method named -main as the entry point for the work that the NSOperation is to complete while running on a background thread. The NSOperationQueue calls this method directly.

Another issue is one of concurrency. If an NSManagedObject is updated on more than one thread, then the results of one or more of those updates is undetermined and unpredictable. Therefore, it is recommended that NSManagedObject instances do not cross thread "boundaries."

9.2 Creating Multiple Contexts

Currently, there is one approved method for using Core Data across multiple threads. This method involves creating a separate NSManagedObjectContext for each thread that will be interacting with Core Data. The creation of the separate context on a background thread is quite straightforward and is nearly identical to the creation of the NSManagedObjectContext on the main thread.

`MultiThreading/PPImportOperation.m`

```
- (NSManagedObjectContext*)newContextToMainStore
{
  NSPersistentStoreCoordinator *coord = nil;
  coord = [appDelegate persistentStoreCoordinator];

  NSManagedObjectContext *moc = [[NSManagedObjectContext alloc] init];
  [moc setPersistentStoreCoordinator:coord];
  return [moc autorelease];
}
```

As shown in the method -newContextToMainStore, we grab a reference to the existing NSPersistentStoreCoordinator and use that in the initialization of a new NSManagedObjectContext.

Although the NSPersistentStoreCoordinator is not thread safe either, the NSManagedObjectContext knows how to lock it properly when in use. Therefore, we can attach as many NSManagedObjectContext objects to a single NSPersistentStoreCoordinator as we want without fear of collision.

Cross-Thread Communication

There is one major catch when standing up multiple NSManagedObjectContext instances. Each instance is unaware of the existence and activity of the other instances. This means that when an NSManagedObject is created, edited, or deleted by one NSManagedObjectContext, the other instances aren't aware of the change.

Fortunately, Apple has given us a relatively easy way to keep all the NSManagedObjectContext instances in sync. Every time that an NSManagedObjectContext completes a save operation, it will broadcast an NSNotification with the key NSManagedObjectContextDidSaveNotification. In addition, the NSNotification instance will contain all the information about what is occurring in that save.

To complement this NSNotification broadcast, the NSManagedObjectContext has a method that is designed to consume this NSNotification and update itself based on its contents. This method, -mergeChangesFromContextDidSaveNotification:, will update the NSManagedObjectContext with the changes and will also notify any observers of those changes. This means that our main NSManagedObjectContext can be updated with a single call whenever the background NSManagedObjectContext instances perform a save, and our user interface will be updated automatically.

9.3 Exporting Recipes

In this first demonstration of multithreading, we will be adding the ability to export recipes from our database so that they can be shared. In this new section of the application, we will be creating an NSOperation, which will create its own NSManagedObjectContext, and use it to copy the selected recipes into a new NSManagedObjectContext, which is then saved to a location specified by the user.

To implement this addition to our application, we need to make a few changes to the user interface. We want to add a menu item for the user to select when they want to export a recipe, and we want to display a sheet for the user to select which recipe(s) they want to extract.

Before we can add the menu item, we want to add a method to the AppDelegate header for the menu item to be bound to.

`MultiThreading/AppDelegate.h`

```
- (IBAction)exportRecipes:(id)sender;
- (IBAction)exportApproved:(id)sender;
- (IBAction)exportCancelled:(id)sender;
```

We have added three new methods to our AppDelegate. The first, -exportRecipes:, will be called by the new menu item and will display our sheet allowing the user to select which recipe(s) to export. The second, -exportApproved:, will be called from the export button on that sheet, and the third, -exportCancelled:, will be called from the cancel button of that same sheet.

Updating the User Interface

To kick off the export, the user will select a menu item under the File menu.

We will bind this menu item to the -exportRecipes: method that we added to our AppDelegate header (shown in Figure 9.5, on page 169). When this menu item is selected, we want a sheet to drop down with a list that the user can select from. To do this, we will need to add a new NSArrayController to our xib file, naming it export list, and bind it to our AppDelegate. We will also need to create a new NSPanel, named Export

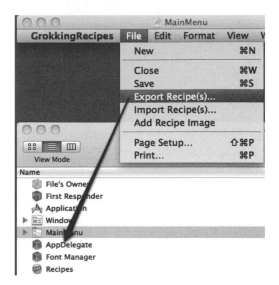

Figure 9.1: LINKING THE IMPORT MENU ITEM

Sheet, that will be used as our sheet. On this sheet, we will add an NSTableView and two buttons, one named Cancel and the other named Export, as demonstrated in Figure 9.2, on the following page.

Note that we have two columns in the table with a checkbox in the first column. The second column is going to display the name of the recipe. We want to bind each of these columns to the export list's NSArrayController that we added earlier. The checkbox column should be bound to the model key path of selected, and the name column should be bound to the model key path of name. Both columns should have their controller key set to arrangedObjects.

The Export button needs to be bound to the -exportApproved: method we added to our AppDelegate. Likewise, the Cancel button needs to be bound to the -exportCancelled: method. The one last change we need to make is to turn off Visible At Launch and Release When Closed. We want to reuse this NSPanel and therefore do not want to release it, and we also do not want it displayed when our application first launches.

Implementing the Export Methods

Now that we have updated our UI, we need to implement the new methods in our AppDelegate.

Chapter 9. Multithreading and Core Data

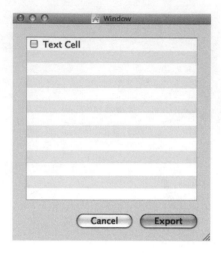

Figure 9.2: NEW NSPANEL FOR THE EXPORT LIST

MultiThreading/AppDelegate.m

```
#pragma mark Export methods
#pragma mark -

- (IBAction)exportRecipes:(id)sender;
{
  NSFetchRequest *request = [[NSFetchRequest alloc] init];
  NSManagedObjectContext *moc = [self managedObjectContext];
  [request setEntity:[NSEntityDescription entityForName:@"Recipe"
                                inManagedObjectContext:moc]];
  NSError *error = nil;
  NSArray *recipes = [moc executeFetchRequest:request
                                        error:&error];
  if (error) {
    [NSApp presentError:error];
    return;
  }
}
```

The first step in our export is to grab all the recipes. We accomplish this by doing an NSFetchRequest with the Recipe entity and without a predicate. This will give us an NSArray of all the recipes in our NSManagedObjectContext.

MultiThreading/AppDelegate.m

```
NSMutableArray *exportList = [NSMutableArray array];
for (NSManagedObject *recipe in recipes) {
  NSMutableDictionary *entry = [NSMutableDictionary dictionary];
```

```
    [entry setValue:[NSNumber numberWithBool:NO]
            forKey:@"selected"];
    [entry setValue:[recipe valueForKey:@"name"]
            forKey:@"name"];
    [entry setValue:[recipe objectID]
            forKey:@"objectID"];
    [exportList addObject:entry];
}
[exportArrayController setContent:exportList];
```

Now that we have an NSArray of the recipes, we need to store the recipes in our NSArrayController. However, the Recipe entity does not have any way to specify whether it has been selected, so we will load NSDictionary objects into the NSArrayController instead. Therefore, we will create a new NSMutableArray and start looping over the results of our fetch. For each result, we grab the name and the NSManagedObjectID and store both in a new NSMutableDictionary. We also need to add an NSNumber into the NSMutableDictionary set to NO with the key selected. This NSNumber will be used to determine whether the user has selected that recipe.

Once we have added all the recipes to the NSMutableArray, we can then set it as the content of the NSArrayController that is being used to display the export list in our UI. Calling the -setContent: of the NSArrayController will trigger the KVO and cause the NSTableView to be updated for us.

`MultiThreading/AppDelegate.m`

```
[NSApp beginSheet:exportSheet
   modalForWindow:window
    modalDelegate:nil
   didEndSelector:NULL
      contextInfo:nil];
```

Once the NSArrayController has been loaded, we need to display the sheet. This is performed by a call to the shared NSApplication. Now when our user selects Export Recipe(s) from the File menu, they will be presented with a sheet to select from, as shown in Figure 9.3, on the next page.

The -exportCancelled: method involves only closing the sheet and returning control to the user. Doing this requires two calls in the resulting method.

`MultiThreading/AppDelegate.m`

```
- (IBAction)exportCancelled:(id)sender;
{
  [exportSheet orderOut:sender];
  [NSApp endSheet:exportSheet];
  [exportArrayController setContent:nil];
}
```

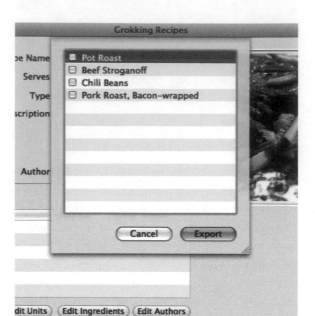

Figure 9.3: DISPLAYING THE EXPORT SHEET

The -exportApproved: method is also quite brief. In this method we want to also close the sheet, but we want to then present an NSSavePanel as a sheet to the user so that they can tell us where to save the exported recipes. Since the NSSavePanel will be asynchronous as a sheet, we need to pass along the selected recipe's NSManagedObjectID objects so that the callback can use them to do the actual export.

MultiThreading/AppDelegate.m
```
- (IBAction)exportApproved:(id)sender;
{
  [exportSheet orderOut:sender];
  [NSApp endSheet:exportSheet];

  NSArray *content = [exportArrayController content];
  NSPredicate *pred = [NSPredicate predicateWithFormat:@"selected == YES"];
  NSArray *filtered = [content filteredArrayUsingPredicate:pred];
  NSArray *exportIDs = [filtered valueForKeyPath:@"objectID"];

  NSSavePanel *savePanel = [NSSavePanel savePanel];
  [savePanel setExtensionHidden:YES];
  [savePanel setRequiredFileType:@"grx"];
  [savePanel setCanSelectHiddenExtension:NO];
```

```
SEL select = @selector(exportSaveDidEnd:returnCode:contextInfo:);
[savePanel beginSheetForDirectory:nil
                             file:nil
                   modalForWindow:window
                    modalDelegate:self
                    didEndSelector:select
                       contextInfo:[exportIDs retain]];
[exportArrayController setContent:nil];
}
```

Kicking Off the NSOperation

The last change we need to make to the AppDelegate is the callback for our NSSavePanel. In this last method, we are grabbing both the filename and the context from the NSSavePanel and constructing an instance of a new class: PPExportOperation. During the initialization, we are passing in a reference to the AppDelegate, the save path, and the NSManaged-ObjectID objects for the recipes that need to be exported. After the PPExportOperation has been constructed, we can hand it off to an NSOperationQueue. This will cause the PPExportOperation to be run on another thread, allowing the UI to proceed.

MultiThreading/AppDelegate.m

```
- (void)exportSaveDidEnd:(NSSavePanel*)savePanel
              returnCode:(NSInteger)returnCode
             contextInfo:(NSArray*)exportIDs
{
  if (returnCode == NSCancelButton) {
    [exportIDs release];
    return;
  }

  PPExportOperation *op = nil;
  op = [[PPExportOperation alloc] initWithDelegate:self
                                        objectIDs:exportIDs
                                     saveFilePath:[savePanel filename]];

  if (!genericOperationQueue) {
    genericOperationQueue = [[NSOperationQueue alloc] init];
  }

  [genericOperationQueue addOperation:op];
  [exportIDs release];
  [op release];
}
```

> ### Making the Copy One-Way
>
> When we are performing this copy, it would be very easy to copy the entire Core Data repository. Because all our objects are linked via two-way relationships, if we built a recursive method to copy the objects and follow their relationships, we would end up with a complete duplicate of all the recipes.
>
> To prevent that, we added a check into each object copy. Whenever it follows a relationship, it first checks to make sure that the destination entity of that relationship is not the same entity as the parent entity that called it. By doing this, we guarantee that the entity tree is copied in only one direction, as shown in Figure 9.4, on the facing page

Although quite a bit of code is involved in the export operation, we will touch on only a couple parts of it that are relevant to the manipulation of the Core Data elements.

MultiThreading/PPExportOperation.m

```
- (void)main
{
  NSManagedObjectContext *exportMOC = [self managedObjectContext];
  if (!exportMOC) return;

  NSPersistentStoreCoordinator *sourceStore = nil;
  sourceStore = [appDelegate persistentStoreCoordinator];
  NSManagedObjectContext *sourceMOC = [[NSManagedObjectContext alloc] init];
  [sourceMOC setPersistentStoreCoordinator:sourceStore];
```

Before we can start the export, we can build the NSManagedObjectContext for the export file. Once we have constructed the new Core Data stack for the export file, the next step is to construct a new NSManagedObjectContext that is associated with the primary NSPersistentStoreCoordinator for the application. To this end, we obtain a reference to the primary NSPersistentStoreCoordinator from the AppDelegate reference that was passed in when we initialized the NSOperation. With that reference obtained, we next instantiate a new NSManagedObjectContext and set the NSPersistentStoreCoordinator. We now have two NSManagedObjectContext instances talking to the same NSPersistentStoreCoordinator.

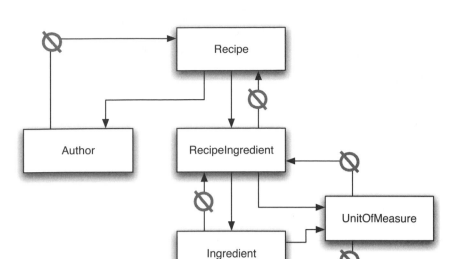

Figure 9.4: The flow of the copy

MultiThreading/PPExportOperation.m

```
for (NSManagedObjectID *objectID in [self objectIDs]) {
  NSManagedObject *object = [sourceMOC objectWithID:objectID];
  [self copyObject:object
         toContext:exportMOC
             parent:nil]];
}
[sourceMOC release], sourceMOC = nil;
```

Although this part of the -main performs all the work for the export, it is actually very quick. Since we are not writing anything to disk yet and the Recipe objects are already in memory, we are performing this section of code very quickly. This copy operation will duplicate not only the Recipe entity that we are exporting but all the other entities associated with that recipe. Once all the selected Recipe objects have been copied into the new NSManagedObjectContext, it is time to unlock the primary NSManagedObjectContext.

MultiThreading/PPExportOperation.m

```
  NSError *error = nil;
  if (![exportMOC save:&error]) {
    [NSApp presentError:error];
  }
}
```

Once the copy is complete, we can write the new context to disk. If there is an error during the save, we notify the user and finish the operation. Once the -main method exits, the instance will be released by the NSOperationQueue, and all the temporary objects we used will be freed in our -dealloc method.

9.4 Importing Recipes

Being able to export recipes is a great addition to our application. It not only makes it easier for our users to share recipes, but it also promotes the application itself. Existing users can share their recipes with new users, and those new users will have to use our application to view the recipes. It's a great little micro market of its own. However, users also need the ability to import these recipes to complete the circuit.

While implementing the import feature, we will also build a second NSManagedObjectContext. This will allow us to add records as needed, and when we are done with our manipulations, we can notify the main thread of those changes. By putting the import on a separate thread, the user can continue to operate the UI while the import is occurring. When we are done with the import, the user will just see the recipes added.

As with the earlier export operation, quite a bit of code is involved in the import. I recommend reviewing the full process because we will be touching only lightly on the mechanics here. The full implementation of this process is included with the example code.

Updating the User Interface

Adding the import functionality requires a minor change to the user interface. Like the export feature, we want to add another NSMenuItem to the File menu called Import Recipe(s). We also want to bind that NSMenuItem to a new method in our AppDelegate called -importRecipes: (see Figure 9.5, on the next page). In that method, we want to display an NSOpenPanel to the user as a sheet and force it to allow only selection of our export records.

MultiThreading/AppDelegate.m

```
#pragma mark Import methods
#pragma mark -
```

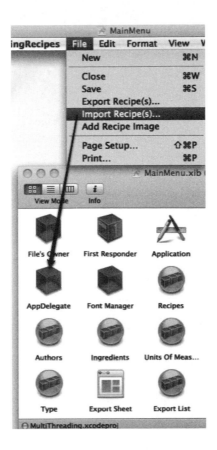

Figure 9.5: LINKING THE IMPORT MENU ITEM

```objc
- (IBAction)importRecipes:(id)sender;
{
  NSOpenPanel *openPanel = [NSOpenPanel openPanel];
  [openPanel setCanChooseDirectories:NO];
  [openPanel setCanCreateDirectories:NO];
  [openPanel setRequiredFileType:@"grx"];

  SEL selector = @selector(importSheetDidEnd:returnCode:context:);
  [openPanel beginSheetForDirectory:nil
                               file:nil
                      modalForWindow:window
                       modalDelegate:self
                      didEndSelector:selector
                         contextInfo:nil];
}
```

For the import, there is nothing we need to do before showing the NSOpenPanel to the user. All of the work is done after our user has selected a file to import.

```
MultiThreading/AppDelegate.m
- (void)importSheetDidEnd:(NSOpenPanel*)openPanel
                returnCode:(NSInteger)returnCode
                   context:(void*)context
{
  if (returnCode == NSCancelButton) return;

  PPImportOperation *op = nil;
  op = [[PPImportOperation alloc] initWithDelegate:self
                                          filePath:[openPanel filename]];

  if (!genericOperationQueue) {
    genericOperationQueue = [[NSOperationQueue alloc] init];
  }

  [genericOperationQueue addOperation:op];
  [op release], op = nil;
}
```

When the NSOpenPanel calls back to our AppDelegate, we first check to see whether the user canceled the sheet. If they did not, then we grab the filename from the NSOpenPanel and pass it into a new instance of PPImportOperation along with a reference to the AppDelegate. After the PPImportOperation has been initialized, we hand it off to the NSOperationQueue and return control to the user. The rest of the import is performed within the PPImportOperation.

Performing the Import Operation

The import is a fair bit more complicated than the export. Although the concept is the same, we are copying NSManagedObject objects from one NSManagedObjectContext to another. In this case, we need to worry about certain objects being duplicated. We do not care if the Recipe and RecipeIngredient objects are duplicated, but we don't want to duplicate UnitOfMeasure, Author, or Ingredient entities. Therefore, as part of the import, whenever one of these objects is run across, it is searched for in the primary NSManagedObjectContext before being created.

To help keep the -main as clean as possible, a lot of the initialization is going to be done in the -initWithDelegate:filePath: instead.

`MultiThreading/PPImportOperation.m`

```
- (id)initWithDelegate:(AppDelegate*)delegate
              filePath:(NSString*)filePath
{
  if (!(self = [super init])) return nil;

  appDelegate = delegate;

  [self setFilePath:filePath];
  [self setImportContext:[self managedObjectContext]];
  NSManagedObjectContext *mainMOC = [self newContextToMainStore];
  NSNotificationCenter *center = [NSNotificationCenter defaultCenter];
  [center addObserver:self
             selector:@selector(contextDidSave:)
                 name:NSManagedObjectContextDidSaveNotification
               object:mainMOC];
  [self setMainContext:mainMOC];
  [self setLookup:[NSMutableDictionary dictionary]];
  return self;
}
```

Once the (super init) has returned, we set the filePath to an ivar, construct an NSManagedObjectContext for it, and set that to another ivar. Once we have the NSManagedObjectContext instantiated for the file to be imported, we also want to start listening for NSNotification broadcasts from that NSManagedObjectContext.

`MultiThreading/PPImportOperation.m`

```
- (void)main
{
  NSFetchRequest *request = [[NSFetchRequest alloc] init];
  [request setEntity:[NSEntityDescription entityForName:@"Recipe"
                                 inManagedObjectContext:[self importContext]]];

  NSError *error = nil;
  NSArray *incomingRecipes = [[self importContext] executeFetchRequest:request
                                                                error:&error];
  [request release], request = nil;
  if (error) {
    [NSApp presentError:error];
    return;
  }
```

At the start of our -main, we need to grab a reference to all the Recipe entities that are in the import file. Since we have an NSManagedObjectContext attached to the file, we need to perform an NSFetchRequest against that NSManagedObjectContext and retrieve an array of NSManagedObject references for the Recipe objects.

MultiThreading/PPImportOperation.m

```
NSAutoreleasePool *pool = [[NSAutoreleasePool alloc] init];
for (NSManagedObject *recipe in incomingRecipes) {
  [self copyRecipe:recipe];
  [pool drain], pool = nil;
  pool = [[NSAutoreleasePool alloc] init];
}
[pool drain], pool = nil;
```

Once we have all the recipes, we need to loop over them and copy each one to the main NSManagedObjectContext. This copy operation is fairly complicated, but the basic flow is this:

1. Copy the Recipe entity and its property attributes.

2. Copy each relationship, searching for existing objects by name if they are not RecipeIngredients. If they are RecipeIngrdients, copy them without searching.

3. For each object in the relationship, copy its relationships, taking care to never copy parent objects.

This copy is one-way, as discussed in the sidebar on page 166. Once the copy is complete, we need to save the main NSManagedObjectContext and get ready to update the main thread and its NSManagedObjectContext.

MultiThreading/PPImportOperation.m

```
error = nil;
if (![[self mainContext] save:&error]) {
  [NSApp presentError:error];
  return;
}
```

Once we have completed the import, it is time to save the context and confirm that it was successful. Once the save is complete, we can exit the -main method and complete the NSOperation. The only question that remains is, how do we update the main NSManagedObjectContext and thereby the UI?

When we wrote the -initWithDelegate:filePath:, we added the NSOperation as an observer to its own NSManagedObjectContextDidSaveNotification broadcasts. When we performed the -save: in the -main method, the notification was automatically fired. To update the main NSManagedObjectContext, we need to forward that notification along.

MultiThreading/PPImportOperation.m

```
- (void)contextDidSave:(NSNotification*)notification
{
  SEL selector = @selector(mergeChangesFromContextDidSaveNotification:);
  [[appDelegate managedObjectContext] performSelectorOnMainThread:selector
                                          withObject:notification
                                          waitUntilDone:YES];
}
```

In the implementation of the -contextDidSave: method, we only need to
pass along the notification to the main NSManagedObjectContext and
make sure that the -mergeChangesFromContextDidSaveNotification: is
called on the main thread. Once that call is complete, the main NSManagedObjectContext will be up-to-date as will any observers it has, including the user interface.

9.5 The Recursive Copy Reviewed

Although not strictly relevant to the subject of multithreading, it is valuable to review how the recursive copy that is used in these operations
works. Of the two, the recursive copy in the PPImportOperation is more
complex, so we will review that one.

-copyRecipe:

MultiThreading/PPImportOperation.m

```
- (void)copyRecipe:(NSManagedObject*)recipe
{
  NSString *entityName = [[recipe entity] name];

  NSManagedObject *newObject = [NSEntityDescription
                                insertNewObjectForEntityForName:entityName
                                inManagedObjectContext:[self mainContext]];

  [[self lookup] setObject:newObject forKey:[recipe objectID]];

  //Catch 22  Need to copy properties before changing the name but that
  //loads it into the context causing an infinite loop
  [self copyPropertiesFromObject:recipe toObject:newObject parent:entityName];
  [newObject setValue:@"untitled recipe" forKey:@"name"];

  NSUInteger index = 1;
  NSString *newName = [recipe valueForKey:@"name"];
  while ([self objectOfType:entityName withName:newName]) {
    NSString *origName = [recipe valueForKey:@"name"];
    newName = [NSString stringWithFormat:@"%@-%u", origName, index];
    ++index;
  }
  [newObject setValue:newName forKey:@"name"];
}
```

The recursive copy starts out by copying the Recipe object. Since we know that we will always be copying the Recipe object, there is no check, in the beginning, to see whether it already exists. Therefore, a new NSManagedObject is created on the correct NSManagedObjectContext, and then its properties and relationships are copied, which we will review in a moment.

One thing to note is that as soon as we create the new NSManagedObject, we insert it into the lookup dictionary using the object's NSManagedObjectID as the key. This NSDictionary will be used as a lookup later for relationships.

After the copy is complete, the name of the new Recipe entity is changed to "untitled recipe," and a search is done on the NSManagedObjectContext to see whether another recipe exists with the same name. The name is changed first to ensure that we do not find *this* recipe in that search. If a recipe is found, then we loop over the name, incrementing an index and adding that index to the name in each pass until we find a variant of the name that does not exist. Once that is found, or if the name is not a duplicate, we reset the name onto the NSManagedObject.

-copyPropertiesFromObject:toObject:parent:

This method is at the heart of the recursive copy. There are two parts to the copy operation.

MultiThreading/PPImportOperation.m

```
- (void)copyPropertiesFromObject:(NSManagedObject*)oldObject
                        toObject:(NSManagedObject*)newObject
                          parent:(NSString*)parentEntity
{
  NSString *entityName = [[oldObject entity] name];
  NSArray *attKeys = [[[oldObject entity] attributesByName] allKeys];
  NSDictionary *attributes = [oldObject dictionaryWithValuesForKeys:attKeys];
  [newObject setValuesForKeysWithDictionary:attributes];
```

In the first part of the copy operation, we will retrieve all the names of the attributes in the object. This information is stored in the NSEntityDescription, which can be referenced from the NSManagedObject via the -entity method. Once we have an NSArray of all the attribute names, we can get their values stored in an NSDictionary. We can then pass this dictionary to the new NSManagedObject and thereby update all of its attributes.

```
MultiThreading/PPImportOperation.m
  id oldDestObject = nil;
  id temp = nil;
  NSDictionary *relationships = [[oldObject entity] relationshipsByName];
  for (NSString *key in [relationships allKeys]) {
    NSRelationshipDescription *desc = [relationships valueForKey:key];
    NSString *destEntityName = [[desc destinationEntity] name];
    if ([destEntityName isEqualToString:parentEntity]) continue;

    if ([desc isToMany]) {
      NSMutableSet *newDestSet = [NSMutableSet set];
      for (oldDestObject in [oldObject valueForKey:key]) {
        temp = [[self lookup] objectForKey:[oldDestObject objectID]];
        if (!temp) {
          temp = [self associateObject:oldDestObject
                                parent:entityName];
        }
        [newDestSet addObject:temp];
      }
      [newObject setValue:newDestSet forKey:key];
    } else {
      oldDestObject = [oldObject valueForKey:key];
      if (!oldDestObject) continue;
      temp = [[self lookup] objectForKey:[oldDestObject objectID]];
      if (!temp) {
        temp = [self associateObject:oldDestObject
                              parent:entityName];
      }
      [newObject setValue:temp forKey:key];
    }
  }
]
}
```

The second half of the copy is quite a bit more complicated. The first issue is that a relationship can be pointing to one object or multiple objects, and each of those possibilities needs to be handled differently. Second, the object on the other end of that relationship may or may not exist. If the destination object exists, then we can just set the relationship. If it does not exist, then we need to create it, which is done in the -associateObject:parent: method discussed in a moment. It is here that we use the lookup dictionary. By using the NSManagedObjectID as the key, we can ensure that different relationships pointing to the same object remain intact.

One important thing to note here is the parentEntity variable that is being passed in. This variable is checked at the start of each relationship copy. If the destination object for that relationship matches this variable, then the relationship is skipped. This guarantees that the copy is performed only *down* the tree and never back up.

-associateObject:parent:

This method is called from the -copyPropertiesFromObject:toObject:parent: method whenever it fails to find a destination object in the lookup dictionary.

```
MultiThreading/PPImportOperation.m
```
```objc
- (id)associateObject:(NSManagedObject*)object parent:(NSString*)name
{
  NSManagedObjectContext *moc = [self mainContext];
  NSString *entityName = [[object entity] name];
  id temp = nil;

  if ([entityName isEqualToString:@"RecipeIngredient"]) {
    temp = [NSEntityDescription insertNewObjectForEntityForName:entityName
                                  inManagedObjectContext:moc];
    [[self lookup] setObject:temp forKey:[object objectID]];
    [self copyPropertiesFromObject:object toObject:temp parent:name];
    return temp;
  }

  if (temp = [self objectOfType:entityName
                    withName:[object valueForKey:@"name"]]) {
    [[self lookup] setObject:temp forKey:[object objectID]];
    return temp;
  }

  temp = [NSEntityDescription insertNewObjectForEntityForName:entityName
                                inManagedObjectContext:moc];
  [[self lookup] setObject:temp forKey:[object objectID]];
  [self copyPropertiesFromObject:object toObject:temp parent:name];
  return temp;
}
```

In this method, unlike the previous method discussed, we care what kind of entity we are working with. If we are working with a RecipeIngredient, then we know to just blindly create a new object. However, for any other object, we need to first check to see whether it already exists in the NSManagedObjectContext. We do this by calling -objectOfType:withName:, and if it returns a nil, then we need to create a new object. If it returns an NSManagedObject, then we associate that returned object with the original object passed in so that future calls against it will be found in the lookup dictionary.

There are a couple of things to note. First, no matter whether we are creating a new object or associating an existing object, we always store the reference in our lookup dictionary. This makes sure we do not duplicate the work and that we can refresh the object later as needed.

The other important thing to note here is the recursion. If we create a new object, we call copyPropertiesFromObject:toObject:parent: on that object even though that is the method that we just came from. However, because of the parent reference, we guarantee that the copy loop never goes back up the chain.

-objectOfType:withName:

The final method in this copy routine is called from the -associateObject: parent: method. This method determines whether an object already exists in the NSManagedObjectContext to avoid duplication.

MultiThreading/PPImportOperation.m

```
- (id)objectOfType:(NSString*)entityName withName:(NSString*)name
{
  NSFetchRequest *request = [[NSFetchRequest alloc] init];
  [request setEntity:[NSEntityDescription entityForName:entityName
                              inManagedObjectContext:[self mainContext]]];
  [request setPredicate:[NSPredicate predicateWithFormat:@"name = %@", name]];

  NSError *error = nil;
  id result = [[[[self mainContext] executeFetchRequest:request
                                          error:&error] lastObject];
  return result;
}
```

In our data model, almost every object has a name property. Fortunately, in the one case that this is not true, we don't care whether there are duplicate objects. Therefore, this method gets rather heavily used during the import operation to help guarantee that we are not creating more than one object with the same name.

We accomplish this check by creating an NSFetchRequest using the name as the test in the predicate and using the passed-in entityName to construct the NSEntityDescription. We then return the -lastObject of the NSArray returned from the fetch. By using -lastObject, we can avoid having to check the length of the returned array. -lastObject will check the length for us automatically and return a nil if the NSArray has no objects.

9.6 Wrapping Up

In this chapter, we reviewed how to use Core Data in a multithreaded application and added some very useful features to our recipes application. We have learned that each thread needs to have its own NS-ManagedObjectContext and that NSManagedObject instances should never cross threads. We also learned how to send notifications across threads so that changes in one NSManagedObjectContext can be updated in other NSManagedObjectContext instances.

Core Data and iPhone

Core Data is now available on the iPhone. Introduced as part of the iPhone 3.0 SDK, the API is nearly identical to the desktop version. There are, however, some very important differences that we will review in this chapter.

This chapter assumes that you have at least a basic understanding of how code is written for the Cocoa Touch devices and are comfortable with the UIViewController design. If you are not, then I highly recommend reading Bill Dudney and Chris Adamson's *iPhone SDK Development* (also from the Pragmatic Bookshelf) before proceeding with this chapter.

10.1 Similarities and Differences

The Core Data API is nearly identical on both the desktop and Cocoa Touch devices. Of course, "nearly identical" and "identical" are not the same thing. We need to be conscious of a few very important differences between the desktop and Cocoa Touch before designing an application to run on Cocoa Touch.

Creating a New Core Data Cocoa Touch Project

When starting a new Cocoa Touch project, it is possible to add Core Data to many of the existing templates. To do this, select the template that you want to start with, and then select the "Use Core Data for storage" checkbox before progressing in the creation of the template.

To demonstrate using Core Data on the iPhone, we will be using the Navigation-based Application template with the "Use Core Data for storage" box selected, as shown in Figure 10.1, on the next page. We'll start this project in Section 10.4, *Recipes for the iPhone*, on page 190.

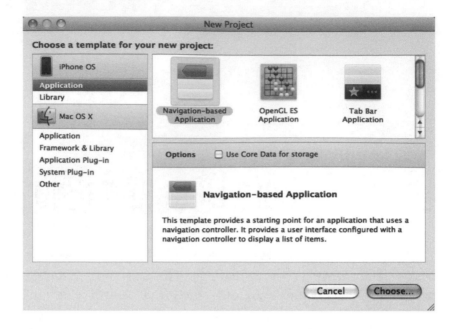

Figure 10.1: IPHONE OS NEW PROJECT DIALOG BOX

Upgrading an Existing Application to Core Data

Many of us have been developing iPhone applications since the SDK's original release, so it is quite likely that you have an existing application that you want to integrate with Core Data. Fortunately, it does not take very much code to build up the Core Data stack in an existing project.

Adding a Data Model to the Project

Just like on the desktop, Core Data on Cocoa Touch requires a data model to define the structure of the data entities. Therefore, the first step is to add a data model to the project by selecting File > New File. Within the dialog box that appears, if we select the Resources section, we can then create a new data model, as shown in Figure 10.2, on the next page.

In addition to creating a new data model, we can also use an existing data model from an existing application. Later in this chapter, in Section 10.4, *Recipes for the iPhone*, on page 190, we use the data model from our desktop recipes application in our new iPhone application. The data models are compatible between the desktop and Cocoa Touch,

Figure 10.2: ADDING A DATA MODEL TO THE PROJECT

which allows us to share not only models but the underling persistent stores as well.

Adding the Core Data Code

Once we have a data model to work with, we next need to add the code to load the Core Data stack. The exact placement of this code depends on the design of your application. Since there are no document-style applications on the iPhone, it is most common to have a single data model and a single persistent store per Cocoa Touch application. Although I still like to put the Core Data code in the application delegate, it might make sense to put it somewhere else. No matter where the code is placed, it is very similar to the desktop. First we need to initialize the data model.

RecipeCT/Classes/AppDelegate.m

```
- (NSManagedObjectModel*)managedObjectModel
{
  if (managedObjectModel) return managedObjectModel;

  NSString *path = [[NSBundle mainBundle] pathForResource:@"DataModel"
                                           ofType:@"momd"];
```

```
  if (!path) {
    path = [[NSBundle mainBundle] pathForResource:@"DataModel"
                                      ofType:@"mom"];
  }
  NSAssert(path != nil, @"Unable to find DataModel in main bundle");
  NSURL *url = [NSURL fileURLWithPath:path];
  managedObjectModel = [[NSManagedObjectModel alloc] initWithContentsOfURL:url];
  return managedObjectModel;
}
```

This should look quite familiar because it is identical to the way you would build the NSManagedObjectModel on the desktop. We get the path for the .mom file (or the .momd if there are multiple versions of the data model) and use it to initialize the NSManagedObjectModel.

RecipeCT/Classes/AppDelegate.m

```
- (NSString*)documentsFolder
{
  NSArray *paths = NSSearchPathForDirectoriesInDomains(NSDocumentDirectory,
                                           NSUserDomainMask, YES);
  NSString *filePath = [paths objectAtIndex:0];
  return filePath;
}
```

Before we construct the NSPersistentStoreCoordinator, we need to decide where to store the persistent store file. On the desktop in an application with a single persistent store, we would save the file to the Application Support folder. However, on Cocoa Touch devices, there is no such location. Instead, each application has its own sandboxed Documents directory designed for the storage of files. This is where we will write our persistent store. Using code similar to what we used on the desktop to find the Application Support folder, we will find the Documents folder specific to our application.

RecipeCT/Classes/AppDelegate.m

```
- (NSPersistentStoreCoordinator*)persistentStoreCoordinator;
{
  if (persistentStoreCoordinator) return persistentStoreCoordinator;

  NSFileManager *fileManager = [NSFileManager defaultManager];
  NSString *docFolder = [self documentsFolder];
  if (![fileManager fileExistsAtPath:docFolder]) {
    [fileManager createDirectoryAtPath:docFolder attributes:nil];
  }

  NSString *filePath = nil;
  filePath = [docFolder stringByAppendingPathComponent:@"recipes.sqlite"];
```

```
  if (![fileManager fileExistsAtPath:filePath]) {
    NSString *defaultDB = [[NSBundle mainBundle] pathForResource:@"recipes"
                                                    ofType:@"sqlite"];
    NSError *error = nil;
    if (![[NSFileManager defaultManager] copyItemAtPath:defaultDB
                                          toPath:filePath
                                          error:&error]) {
      NSLog(@"%@:%s Error copying file %@", [self class], _cmd, error);
    }
  }

  NSURL *url = [NSURL fileURLWithPath:filePath];
  NSManagedObjectModel *mom = [self managedObjectModel];
  persistentStoreCoordinator = [[NSPersistentStoreCoordinator alloc]
                                initWithManagedObjectModel:mom];

  NSError *error = nil;
  if ([persistentStoreCoordinator addPersistentStoreWithType:NSSQLiteStoreType
                                      configuration:nil
                                              URL:url
                                          options:nil
                                          error:&error]) {
    return persistentStoreCoordinator;
  }

  [persistentStoreCoordinator release], persistentStoreCoordinator = nil;
  NSDictionary *ui = [error userInfo];
  if (![ui valueForKey:NSDetailedErrorsKey]) {
    NSLog(@"%@:%s Error adding store %@", [self class], _cmd,
        [error localizedDescription]);
  } else {
    for (NSError *suberror in [ui valueForKey:NSDetailedErrorsKey]) {
      NSLog(@"%@:%s Error: %@", [self class], _cmd,
          [suberror localizedDescription]);
    }
  }
  NSAssert(NO, @"Failed to initialize the persistent store");
  return nil;
}
```

Once we have the NSManagedObjectModel constructed, the next step
is to build the persistent store coordinator. Again, this code is nearly
identical to the desktop version but with a few differences. First, for the
moment, I have turned off the versioning check because we have only
one version on the iPhone. When we release version 2 in the future, we
will need to turn that back on.

The second major difference has to do with default settings. We initially
check for the existence of a database file in the application's Documents directory, but if it does not exist, then we copy one from within

the bundle of the application itself. This gives us a set of "defaults" or "samples" for the user who is accessing the iPhone application for the very first time. By doing this, we can present the user with an inviting list of recipes when they launch our application instead of an empty table view.

```
RecipeCT/Classes/AppDelegate.m
```

```
- (NSManagedObjectContext*)managedObjectContext
{
  if (managedObjectContext) return managedObjectContext;

  NSPersistentStoreCoordinator *coord = [self persistentStoreCoordinator];
  if (!coord) return nil;

  managedObjectContext = [[NSManagedObjectContext alloc] init];
  [managedObjectContext setPersistentStoreCoordinator:coord];

  return managedObjectContext;
}
```

The last method we need to implement is the -managedObjectContext method. Since we did all the hard work either in the -managedObject-Model method or in the -persistentStoreCoordinator method, this method is even simpler than its desktop cousin. We request a reference to the NSPersistentStoreCoordinator, and assuming that it is not nil, we initialize an NSManagedObjectContext, add the NSPersistentStoreCoordinator to it, and return the resulting NSManagedObjectContext. Since we will either have an existing persistent store from the last time the user ran the application or have a default store copied over, there is no need to check the Type table as we have previously. It is guaranteed either to be there or to be intentionally cleared out by the user.

Persistent Store Formats

Similar to Core Data on the desktop, several persistent formats are available on Cocoa Touch devices. However, one format is missing that I have grown to love. The XML format is not available currently on the iPhone. I suspect this is to force us to use something that is far more memory efficient such as the SQLite store. It is also possible that it was skipped because of dependencies on other APIs that are also not available at this time. Whatever the reason, the XML store is not available to us, and we should be using the SQLite store in every situation possible.

Besides the SQLite persistent store format, we also have access to the binary and in-memory formats. However, both of these formats require that the entire object hierarchy be loaded into memory, and that is something we generally cannot afford on a Cocoa Touch device. Therefore, unless there is a very solid design reason to use another store format, SQLite should be used.

10.2 Memory Management

One of the most important differences we need to keep in mind while working with Core Data on the iPhone is the management of memory. Depending on which Cocoa Touch device is targeted, we could have as little as 20MB of memory to work with. This is drastically different from the modern desktop that measures memory in gigabytes! Therefore, Core Data, to be a good citizen on this much smaller device, must handle memory differently.

The best way to handle memory management is to let someone else do it. Fortunately, Apple has stepped up to the plate and done most of the heavy lifting for us. As we will discuss in depth in Section 10.3, *Using the NSFetchedResultsController*, on page 189, the new class, NSFetched-ResultsController, does a lot of the memory management work for us as long as we play by its rules. These rules break down into two separate sections.

Grab Only What You Need

Because we have such a small amount of memory to work with, it is very important that we keep only the entities in memory that we absolutely need for that view. What this means is that if we are working in a view (or a *page*, as some refer to a single screen of information), then we should be retaining only the entities that are needed for that view. In the case of a view that is a table, then that becomes a bit trickier. But fortunately, the NSFetchedResultsController helps us solve that problem as well.

Handling Data Changes

The second rule of working with Core Data on the iPhone has to do with the notification of changes to the data entities. On the desktop our view elements are bound directly to the data entities, and when an entity changes, all the view elements associated with that entity are automatically updated through KVO, as discussed in Chapter 3, *Core Data and Bindings*, on page 27. However, on a CocoaTouch device, those bindings do not currently exist, and updates to visual elements need to be coded.

Figure 10.3: CONTACTS TABLE VIEW

When we're working within one view, this isn't too much of an issue. We have a direct relationship between the view elements being manipulated by the user and the elements displayed by the view. However, what about any other view that exists in the hierarchy that is not currently being displayed but still has elements that are being manipulated?

A good example of this is the Contacts application that exists on every Cocoa Touch device. The primary view for this application is a table listing all the contacts in the database, as shown in Figure 10.3.

In addition to this table view, we also have a detail view that displays a single contact, as shown in Figure 10.4, on the facing page. It is this detail view that handles all the editing of a contact. However, when a detail of that contact gets edited that is also displayed in the parent table view, how does that table view get notified to update its display values?

Figure 10.4: CONTACTS DETAIL VIEW

Without the use of Cocoa Bindings, we need to handle the updates ourselves. We can handle this in several ways, and we will review each of them in Section 10.3, *Data Change Notifications*.

10.3 Data Change Notifications

As we discovered in Section 10.2, *Handling Data Changes*, on page 185, without Cocoa Bindings, we need to consider and design for the situation where our data has changed in one location, and we need to notify another location of that change so that it may also update itself.

However, there are a few catches we have to consider when looking at this problem. The first catch is the one of design elegance. For any application to be elegant on the outside, it must also be elegant on the inside. Therefore, we definitely want to avoid strong references between view controllers.

The second catch has to again do with memory. The Cocoa Touch system has some great memory management features built right into it, and we need to be conscious of them. For example, if we have a UIView-Controller stack that is very deep and we start to hit the memory limits, it is quite possible that the operating system will decide to drop some of our views from memory. If each view is a self-contained island of data, this is generally not a problem. However, if we want to start broadcasting data change notifications back up the stack, this is something we need to be aware of and check for; otherwise, a data notification could cause the entire application to crash.

Using the Delegate Design Pattern

One of the most common solutions to this problem is to use a delegate. In fact, Apple uses this pattern very frequently. Ideally, when using a delegate design, we want to keep a separation between the delegate and the calling object. This will avoid having a strong link between view controllers and allows for the flow of the view controllers to be changed if needed in some future release. With Cocoa Touch, Apple has started using protocols to define delegate methods. Prior to Cocoa Touch (and Objective-C 2.0), it was far more common to add a category to NSObject to define the methods that are called upon the delegate.

With the addition of Objective-C 2.0, we can now have optional methods in a protocol, which makes it easier to use protocols instead of categories. We can now define which methods are required, testing at compile time, and which methods are optional. Previously with categories we had to define which were required and which were optional through runtime checks and documentation.

Unfortunately, using a delegate design does have one fairly major issue. We can have just one delegate being notified when the data changes. If we have a deep stack of view controllers, then we would need to build up a cascade of change notifications up the stack. It's certainly possible but not the most elegant solution in that situation.

Using the NSNotificationCenter

When a delegate won't do, then a notification usually will. The NSNotification API has the advantage of being able to handle multiple observers and notify each of them in turn. In an NSNotification design, each view would add itself as an observer to a specific key. When a notification with that key is broadcast, then the view would receive a callback and be allowed to handle the notification as needed.

The NSNotification API is quite elegant for a number of reasons. Each observer can decide on its own how to handle the notification that it receives. In addition, the object that posts the notification does not need to know anything about the consumers of that notification. It does not even need to know what method is being called on the consumer. The producer simply sends out the notification and carries on. This provides excellent separation of the view controllers.

Using the NSFetchedResultsController

With the release of 3.0 for Cocoa Touch, Apple has provided us with a third solution to this problem. This third solution is provided via the NSFetchedResultsController and is recommended for most standard Cocoa Touch application designs.

The NSFetchedResultsController is specifically designed to manage a result set of entities from an NSManagedObjectContext and provides methods to query the result set for the number of entities and to keep them in order.

In addition, the NSFetchedResultsController also provides means for a UI-ViewController to be notified when any of the entities in the result set are modified including the addition or deletion of entities. The best way to look at the NSFetchedResultsController is as a layer between the NSManagedObjectContext and the UIViewController, as depicted in Figure 10.5, on the next page.

To construct an NSFetchedResultsController, we need to first construct an NSFetchRequest and pass that request into the NSFetchedResultsController. Once that is accomplished, we can query the NSFetchedResultsController for the number of entities in the results and retrieve individual entities.

In our example application, RecipesCT, we will be using the NSFetched-ResultsController to manage the main table view as well as to receive events when the detail view changes one of the entities. This project is discussed in greater detail in Section 10.4, *Recipes for the iPhone*, on the following page.

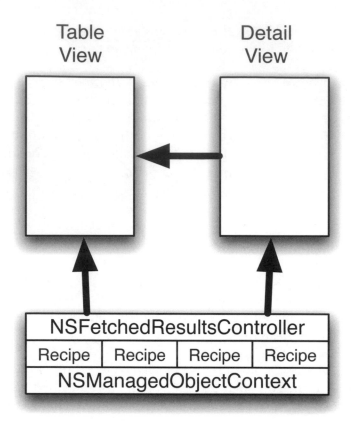

Figure 10.5: NSFetchedResultsController depiction

10.4 Recipes for the iPhone

To demonstrate how to use Core Data in a Cocoa Touch application, we will be taking our recipe application that we have been developing throughout this book and build a Cocoa Touch version. We will start by using the existing data model that we developed for the desktop and copy it to the iPhone. We will also use a SQLite version of our persistent store from the desktop as the sample database for our Cocoa Touch application. Those two steps were already discussed in Section 10.1, *Similarities and Differences*, on page 179.

The next step in our application is to initialize and display the table view, which is the primary view of our application. Once we have completed building the table view, we will then construct a detail view, which will display a single recipe. Although we will not be developing every aspect of this application, we will touch on the key points that involve working with the Core Data portion of the application.

Preparing the NSFetchedResultsController

As soon as the application launches, we want to display a table view of all the available recipes. To do this, we need to construct an NSFetched-ResultsController that manages all the Recipe entities and that the UITable-ViewController will query to display the recipes.

`RecipeCT/Classes/AppDelegate.m`

```
- (void)applicationDidFinishLaunching:(UIApplication*)application
{
  window = [[UIWindow alloc] initWithFrame:[[UIScreen mainScreen] bounds]];

  NSFetchedResultsController *results = [self fetchedResultsController];
  MainViewController *controller - nil;
  controller = [[MainViewController alloc] initWithFetchController:results];

  nav = [[UINavigationController alloc] initWithRootViewController:controller];
  [controller release], controller = nil;
  // Override point for customization after app launch
  [window addSubview:[nav view]];
  [window makeKeyAndVisible];
}
```

Most of this is familiar to you if you've developed a Cocoa Touch application. Once the application has finished launching, we need to build the user interface. To do that, we initialize the window to be the size of the screen, and we then construct our MainViewController, which is the controller managing the main table view. Then we place that MainView-Controller into a UINavigationController so that we can easily transition to the detail view. Once the UINavigationController has been initialized, we add its -view to the window and request that the window become visible.

The one interesting or different part of this method is the initialization of the MainViewController. In this example, it accepts an NSFetchedResults-Controller as part of its initialization. It is expected that the MainView-Controller will retain this NSFetchedResultsController and use it to populate the table view.

The code to construct this NSFetchedResultsController is most interesting.

```
RecipeCT/Classes/AppDelegate.m
```

```objc
- (NSFetchedResultsController*)fetchedResultsController
{
  NSManagedObjectContext *context = [self managedObjectContext];
  NSFetchRequest *fetchRequest = [[NSFetchRequest alloc] init];
  [fetchRequest setEntity:[NSEntityDescription entityForName:@"Recipe"
                                   inManagedObjectContext:context]];
  // Configure the request's entity, and optionally its predicate.
  NSSortDescriptor *sortDescriptor = nil;
  sortDescriptor = [[NSSortDescriptor alloc] initWithKey:@"name" ascending:YES];
  NSArray *sortDescriptors = nil;
  sortDescriptors = [[NSArray alloc] initWithObjects:sortDescriptor, nil];
  [sortDescriptor release], sortDescriptor = nil;
  [fetchRequest setSortDescriptors:sortDescriptors];
  [sortDescriptors release], sortDescriptors = nil;

  NSFetchedResultsController *controller = [[NSFetchedResultsController alloc]
                              initWithFetchRequest:fetchRequest
                              managedObjectContext:context
                              sectionNameKeyPath:nil
                              cacheName:@"Recipe"];

  [fetchRequest release];

  NSError *error = nil;
  BOOL success = [controller performFetch:&error];
  if (!success) {
    NSLog(@"Error fetching request %@", [error localizedDescription]);
  }
  return [controller autorelease];
}
```

As discussed, an NSFetchedResultsController takes an NSFetchRequest as part of its initialization. This NSFetchRequest is used to determine what entities are to be included in the NSFetchedResultsController. In this example, we configure the NSFetchRequest to request all the Recipe entities and to sort them based on the name attribute in ascending order. Once the NSFetchRequest is constructed, we then pass it along to the NSFetchedResultsController along with a reference to the NSManagedObjectContext. We also give it a name for the cache. This cache can be shared across NSFetchedResultsController objects if appropriate, although we will not be doing that in this example.

Once the NSFetchedResultsController has been initialized, we then request that it perform the fetch that will load the entities into memory. It should be noted that the NSFetchedResultsController is very conscious of the available memory on the device, and it will keep only the entities in memory that are currently needed. Therefore, we can expect at this point that it has loaded only the faulted objects into memory and that they are not fully realized yet.

Building the Main Table View

Now that we have the NSFetchedResultsController being passed into the MainViewController, we need to build the main table view. The header for this UITableViewController is very simple. Because we are displaying only a UITableView and nothing else, we can use a UITableViewController instead of its parent, UIViewController. The UITableViewController will handle the reference to the UITableView for us, and it is already declared as both a UITableViewDelegate and a UITableViewDatasource. The resulting header file is as follows:

`RecipeCT/Classes/MainViewController.h`

```
@interface MainViewController : UITableViewController
{
  NSFetchedResultsController *resultsController;
}

@property (retain) NSFetchedResultsController *resultsController;

- (id)initWithFetchController:(NSFetchedResultsController*)controller;

@end
```

In this class, the only thing we are retaining is the NSFetchedResultsController, which will be driving the model for our application. From the header, we can then construct the -initWithFetchController: method, which takes a single parameter, the NSFetchedResultsController constructed in the AppDelegate. Once we have initialized the UITableViewController subclass by calling -initWithStyle: on the superclass, we then set the resultsController property with the passed-in parameter. We also set our MainViewController instance as the delegate to the NSFetchedResultsController so that we receive callbacks when any of the entities managed by the NSFetchedResultsController change.

`RecipeCT/Classes/MainViewController.m`

```
- (id)initWithFetchController:(NSFetchedResultsController*)controller
{
  if (!(self = [super initWithStyle:UITableViewStylePlain])) return nil;

  [self setResultsController:controller];
  [controller setDelegate:self];

  return self;
}
```

The next interesting parts of the MainViewController that we need to implement are the UITableViewDelegate and UITableViewDataSource methods.

Implementing the -numberOfSectionsInTableView: Method

RecipeCT/Classes/MainViewController.m

```
- (NSInteger)numberOfSectionsInTableView:(UITableView*)tableView
{
  return [[[self resultsController] sections] count];
}
```

To be able to ask for the number of rows in a section, the UITableView must first know the number of sections. In this method, we request the sections property of the NSFetchedResultsController, which returns an NSArray of NSFetchedResultsSectionInfo implementations. Since we need to know only the number of sections, we return a call to -count on the resulting NSArray.

Implementing the -tableView:numberOfRowsInSection: Method

One of the first methods that gets called as the table view is being realized is the -tableView:numberOfRowsInSection: method, which tells the UITableView how many rows are going to be displayed.

RecipeCT/Classes/MainViewController.m

```
- (NSInteger)tableView:(UITableView*)table
 numberOfRowsInSection:(NSInteger)section
{
  id <NSFetchedResultsSectionInfo> sectionInfo = nil;
  sectionInfo = [[[self resultsController] sections] objectAtIndex:section];
  return [sectionInfo numberOfObjects];
}
```

In this method, we request a reference to the NSFetchedResultsSectionInfo instance for the specified section. The result is an implementation of the protocol that contains a count of the number of objects in the section as well as a reference to the objects and the name of the section. For this method, we return the result of a call to the numberOfObjects property.

Implementing the -tableView:cellForRowAtIndexPath: Method

The one method that tends to be the most complex in a UITableViewController is the -tableView:cellForRowAtIndexPath: method. This method is responsible for initializing (or dequeuing) the UITableViewCell object that will be displaying a particular row in the table.

RecipeCT/Classes/MainViewController.m

```
- (UITableViewCell*)tableView:(UITableView*)tableView
         cellForRowAtIndexPath:(NSIndexPath*)indexPath
{
  static NSString *cellIdentifier = @"cellIdentifier";
  UITableViewCell *cell = nil;
  cell = [tableView dequeueReusableCellWithIdentifier:cellIdentifier];
  if (!cell) {
    cell = [[[UITableViewCell alloc] initWithStyle:UITableViewCellStyleSubtitle
                                reuseIdentifier:cellIdentifier] autorelease];
    [cell setAccessoryType:UITableViewCellAccessoryDisclosureIndicator];
  }
  [self updateCell:cell fromRecipe:[[self resultsController]
                               objectAtIndexPath:indexPath]];

  return cell;
}
```

Because our table has only one style of row, it makes this class simpler than it tends to be in tables that have multiple row types. We start off by attempting to dequeue a UITableViewCell so that we can reuse it. If there is not one available to dequeue, we construct a new one. Since every cell will display a disclosure indicator, we configure that as part of the initialization of the new cell.

Once the cell is obtained, we need to populate it. Since we will be populating and/or updating cells in more than one location in our controller, the populating of the cell has been abstracted into its own method. Therefore, our -tableView:cellForRowAtIndexPath: needs to obtain a reference to the entity for the row and pass it to the -updateCell:fromRecipe: method.

Because the NSFetchedResultsController class is UITableView aware, we do not need to do any complicated code to obtain the specified object. A single call to -objectAtIndexPath: passing in the referenced NSIndexPath object will yield the relevant recipe.

Implementing the -updateCell:fromRecipe: Method

Whenever a cell is created or updated, its contents need to be configured. Fortunately, we are using one of the new table view cell styles included in 3.0 so that we do not need to do any complicated view construction and layout. However, since the update of a cell can occur in more than one point in our MainViewController, we have move the implementation to its own method.

RecipeCT/Classes/MainViewController.m

```
- (void)updateCell:(UITableViewCell*)cell fromRecipe:(RecipeEntity*)recipe
{
  [[cell textLabel] setText:[recipe name]];
  NSString *text = nil;
  text = [NSString stringWithFormat:@"Serves: %@", [recipe serves]];
  [[cell detailTextLabel] setText:text];
}
```

Because we are using one of the standard cell layouts, the population of the cell merely requires setting the textLabel property and the detailTextLabel property.

Implementing the -controllerWillChangeContent: Method

With the more interesting UITableViewDatasource methods reviewed, the only thing left is to implement the NSFetchedResultsControllerDelegate methods. There are four methods that we need to implement. The first is the -controllerWillChangeContent: method. This method is called once per notification cycle (which can include multiple changes), and it gives us the opportunity to set up our view for the changes that are about to be performed. Because we have only a UITableView displayed, our setup for these changes is very simple.

RecipeCT/Classes/MainViewController.m

```
- (void)controllerWillChangeContent:(NSFetchedResultsController*)controller
{
        [[self tableView] beginUpdates];
}
```

Implementing the -controller:didChangeObject:atIndexPath:forChangeType:newIndexPath: Method

This method is where the meat of the NSFetchedResultsController lies. Whenever an entity is inserted, deleted, changed, or moved, this method will be called. The exact firing of this method occurs after the changes have been saved via the -save: method of the NSManagedObjectContext. Once that occurs, each change is then passed through this method.

RecipeCT/Classes/MainViewController.m

```
- (void)controller:(NSFetchedResultsController*)controller
   didChangeObject:(id)anObject
       atIndexPath:(NSIndexPath*)indexPath
     forChangeType:(NSFetchedResultsChangeType)type
      newIndexPath:(NSIndexPath*)newIndexPath
{
  NSArray *paths = [NSArray arrayWithObject:newIndexPath];
```

```
    NSIndexSet *section = [NSIndexSet indexSetWithIndex:[newIndexPath section]];

        switch (type) {
            case NSFetchedResultsChangeInsert:
                [[self tableView] insertRowsAtIndexPaths:paths
                    withRowAnimation:UITableViewRowAnimationFade];
                break;
            case NSFetchedResultsChangeDelete:
                [[self tableView] deleteRowsAtIndexPaths:paths
                    withRowAnimation:UITableViewRowAnimationFade];
                break;
            case NSFetchedResultsChangeMove:
                [[self tableView] deleteRowsAtIndexPaths:paths
                    withRowAnimation:UITableViewRowAnimationFade];
                [[self tableView] reloadSections:section
                withRowAnimation:UITableViewRowAnimationFade];
                break;
            case NSFetchedResultsChangeUpdate:
    [self updateCell:[[self tableView] cellForRowAtIndexPath:indexPath]
        fromRecipe:[[self resultsController] objectAtIndexPath:indexPath]];
                break;
        }
}
```

For each change, we first determine what type of change has occurred. If an insert or deletion has occurred, then we pass that information onto the UITableView so that the UITableView can then handle the change. In the case of an insertion, the table view would then query the -tableView:numberOfRowsInSection: and -tableView:cellForRowAtIndexPath: methods, respectively. In each of those cases, the UITableView will animate the row change if it is visible on the screen.

In the case of a row being moved (as would occur if the sort property changed sufficiently to warrant a reorder), the UITableView would handle the animation of the rows changing position (again, if they are currently visible on the screen).

In the last possible situation, a change to the properties of the entity, we call our -updateCell:fromRecipe: method and pass it the relevant Recipe entity and UITableViewCell.

Implementing the -controller:didChangeSection:atIndex:forChange-Type: Method

In addition to changing entities, it is also possible that a change in the NSFetchedResultsController could result in a change to the number of sections. For example, if each section represented a letter in the alphabet and we add a new recipe that is the first for that letter, it could cause a new section to be created. Likewise, if we removed the last recipe for a letter, that would cause a section to be deleted.

When a situation occurs that causes a section to be added or removed, a call to the -controller:didChangeSection:atIndex:forChangeType: method will occur. Like the -controller:didChangeObject:atIndexPath:forChange-Type:indexPath: method, we handle calls to this method by determining what type of change is occurring. In both cases, regardless of whether it is a deletion or insertion, we are passing only that information to the UITableView so that it can update the display.

RecipeCT/Classes/MainViewController.m

```
- (void)controller:(NSFetchedResultsController*)controller
  didChangeSection:(id <NSFetchedResultsSectionInfo>)sectionInfo
          atIndex:(NSUInteger)sectionIndex
     forChangeType:(NSFetchedResultsChangeType)type
{
  NSIndexSet *sections = [NSIndexSet indexSetWithIndex:sectionIndex];

        switch (type) {
                case NSFetchedResultsChangeInsert:
                        [[self tableView] insertSections:sections
                          withRowAnimation:UITableViewRowAnimationFade];
                        break;
                case NSFetchedResultsChangeDelete:
                        [[self tableView] deleteSections:sections
                          withRowAnimation:UITableViewRowAnimationFade];
                        break;
        }
}
```

Implementing the -controllerDidChangeContent: Method

The final method that we need to implement is the -controllerDidChange-Content method. Like its partner method, -controllerWillChangeContent:, this method is called once all the changes for the current cycle are completed. For our MainViewController, we need to notify the UITableView that all the changes are complete and it can begin displaying the changes. Note that since all changes to this table view can occur only while the table view is off-screen (only the detail view is editable), there will not be any animation occurring. The UITableView will update its state, but the actual drawing will occur once the UITableView reappears on the screen.

Once the MainViewController is finished, the resulting view should look similar to Figure 10.6, on the facing page. Although we did not review every method needed to complete this view, we did touch on each view

Figure 10.6: COCOA TOUCH RECIPES APPLICATION TABLE VIEW

that is impacted by Core Data. The rest of the methods are implemented in the included example code.

Building the Detail View Controller

The good news is that nearly all the interaction with Core Data is complete. The bad news is that the detail view has the most complex user interface code in the application. Although we are not implementing the entire user interface in this example, there is still quite a bit of code dealing with the editing of fields.

The basic design of the detail view is shown in Figure 10.7, on the next page. The primary section of the view is a table view along with a custom header view. Within the header view is a UIImageView, a UI-Label, and a UITextField. The name of the recipe is contained within the UITextField, which is disabled by default. When the edit button is clicked,

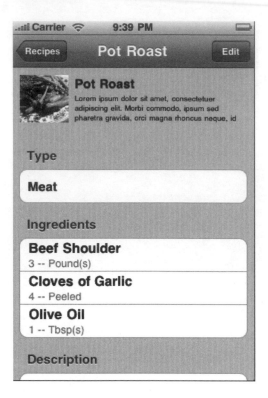

Figure 10.7: COCOA TOUCH RECIPES APPLICATION DETAIL VIEW

the UITextField in the header is enabled so that the user can change the name of the recipe.

If we were to complete this application, there would be a lot more editing capabilities. However, the code is kept to a minimum to help keep the focus on the Core Data changes.

Implementing the -setEditing:animated: Method

All the interaction with the Core Data underpinnings occurs in the -setEditing:animated: method. In this method, in addition to flipping the UITextField between enabled and nonenabled, we also have a check at the very end of the method. If we are going from an edited state to a nonedited state, then the method will perform a save on the NSManagedObjectContext. It is this save that triggers the notifications to the parent table view and causes the updates.

RecipeCT/Classes/RecipeDetailViewController.m

```
- (void)setEditing:(BOOL)editing animated:(BOOL)animated
{
  [super setEditing:editing animated:animated];
  [self.navigationItem setHidesBackButton:editing animated:YES];

  [[self titleLabel] setEnabled:editing];

      if (editing) return;
  NSManagedObjectContext *context = recipe.managedObjectContext;
  NSError *error = nil;
  if ([context save:&error]) return;

  NSLog(@"save error %@, %@", error, [error userInfo]);
  exit(-1); // Fail
}
```

Because we are using an NSFetchedResultsController, it automatically
monitors the NSManagedObjectContext for changes and broadcasts
them to its delegate. Therefore, a simple save of the NSManagedObject-
Context automatically takes care of any change notifications in the other
view controllers.

Overview

In this section, we looked into the impacts that adding Core Data to a
Cocoa Touch application has. Similar to the desktop, Core Data helps to
eliminate a large portion of the code dealing with the object hierarchy
and persisting data to disk. By adding Core Data to a Cocoa Touch
project, we can further reduce the amount of code required to develop
an application and reduce the time to market even further.

10.5 Going Further

Because of our focus purely on Core Data in this chapter, we did not
cover all aspects of this application. We also did not complete the application and make it consumer ready.

Interestingly enough, with the release of v3.0 for Cocoa Touch, Apple
also released a sample recipes application for the iPhone that uses Core
Data. This application is available to everyone who has an iPhone developer account, and I highly recommend reviewing the solutions provided
in that project.

Chapter 11

Recipe: Distributed Core Data

Imagine if all the users in a family had our recipe application and wanted to be able to see everyone else's recipes. You can probably come up with many such scenarios for sharing data across a local area network. If your application sits on a user's desktop and laptop, then there is a fair chance that the user wants to keep that data in sync. Of course, this can be done with a form of cloud syncing, but imagine a small office environment or family of computers. Not every user has the same cloud account (whether it be MobileMe, Dropbox, or some other cloud storage), and you may not want to share the entire data set to every user. Being able to set up a local area sharing can solve the need to share partial or complete data in a local environment.

Core Data is generally considered to be a single-user/single-application persistent store. However, as we explored in Chapter 10, *Core Data and iPhone*, on page 179, Core Data can be used beyond the single-user/single-application design. In this chapter, we are going to explore using Core Data with distributed objects. Distributed objects enable a Cocoa application to call an object in a different Cocoa application (or a different thread in the same application). The applications can even be running on different computers on a network.

To take this idea one step further, we are going to add Bonjour into the design. Bonjour, also known as *zero-configuration networking*, enables automatic discovery of computers, devices, and services on IP networks. With this combination, we can provide access to a Core Data repository to any client on the network "automatically" without user interaction.

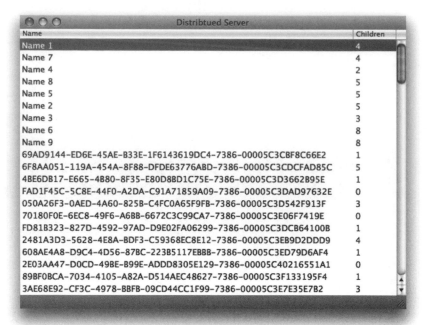

Figure 11.1: DISTRIBUTED SERVER UI

Before we go into the details, I want to mention the cons for this design.

- Scalability: This design does not scale very well at all. When we are working with a couple of clients on a network, then it will perform just fine. When we start scaling it to half a dozen or more clients, it starts to slow down very quickly. There are optimizations that we can do, but if you have more than a couple of clients, you should use a full database solution instead of Core Data.

- Threading: Although all the calls to the server are performed on the main thread, calls within objects passed by reference are not by their very nature. Therefore, if we pass an NSManagedObject by reference to a client and that client makes a change to the NSManagedObject, we are in a worst-case situation with regard to threading.

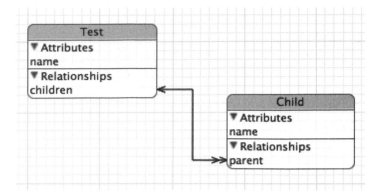

Figure 11.2: DISTRIBUTED SERVER DATA MODEL

11.1 Building the Server

In a normal client-server application, the server would be a background or GUI-less application. In this demonstration, we are going to start with a normal single persistent store Cocoa application instead. There is no benefit to having a UI for a server in a production environment, but for testing, it is useful to see the activity on the server. Therefore, we start with creating a Core Data Cocoa application called Distributed-CDServer. The user interface for the server is a single window with a table view displaying the list of items in the Core Data persistent store, as shown in Figure 11.1, on the preceding page.

The data model for this example is composed of two entities. The top-level entity is named Test and has two properties: name and children. The second entity is called Child and also has two properties: name and parent. The two objects share a many-to-one relationship between the properties children and parent. The resulting model is shown in Figure 11.2.

Distributed Objects Protocol

When I am working with distributed objects, I prefer to contain the contract between the client and the server within a protocol. For this application, we are going to have a few methods that the clients can use to query the server, but we are not going to have any server to client queries.

The resulting protocol is as follows:

`DistributedCDServer/PPDistributedProtocol.h`

```
#define kDomainName @"local."
#define kServiceName @"_pragProgExample._tcp"

@protocol PPDistributedProtocol

- (oneway void)ping;

- (byref NSManagedObject*)createObject;
- (byref NSManagedObject*)createChildForObject:(byref NSManagedObject*)parent;
- (oneway void)deleteObject:(byref NSManagedObject*)object;
- (byref NSArray*)allObjects;
- (byref NSArray*)objectsOfName:(bycopy NSString*)name
                withPredicate:(bycopy NSPredicate*)predicate;

@end
```

When we are working with distributed objects, we need to define how nonscalar attributes are handled.[1] In our protocol, we are passing most of the objects byref, which means that an NSDistantObject is created on the receiver as a proxy to the object that is residing on the server. This is different from bycopy, which will make a copy of the object on the receiving end. One of the interesting differences between these is that KVO works across a distributed object when it is passed byref. This will be demonstrated as we build the application.

Broadcasting the Service

Distributed objects work by using good old Unix sockets. Fortunately, these are wrapped with NSSocketPort for us so that we do not need to use the raw C functions and all the complexity that entails. To use sockets, we need to know the address and port of the socket to talk to. This can be entered by the user, which is a suboptimal experience, or we can discover it using Bonjour. To use Bonjour, we need to set up a broadcast on the server for the client to discover.

`DistributedCDServer/AppDelegate.m`

```
- (void)startBroadcasting
{
  receiveSocket = [[NSSocketPort alloc] init];
  int receivePort = [self portFromSocket:receiveSocket];

  myConnection = [[NSConnection alloc] initWithReceivePort:receiveSocket
                                                  sendPort:nil];
```

---

1. These are discussed in depth in Apple's documentation.

```
    [myConnection setRootObject:self];

    myService = [[NSNetService alloc] initWithDomain:kDomainName
                                        type:kServiceName
                                        name:kServerName
                                        port:receivePort];

    [myService setDelegate:self];
    [myService publish];
}
```

In the -startBroadcasting method, we first initialize a new NSSocketPort. When we use the default -init method, the NSSocketPort will choose a random open port for us to use. However, we need to broadcast this port information as part of the Bonjour service. Therefore, we need to extract the port information from the NSSocketPort object. In a production environment, we probably want to define a port to use instead of selecting one at random.

`DistributedCDServer/AppDelegate.m`

```
- (int)portFromSocket:(NSSocketPort*)socket
{
  struct sockaddr *address = (struct sockaddr*)[[receiveSocket address] bytes];
  uint16_t port;

  if (address->sa_family == AF_INET) {
    port = ntohs(((struct sockaddr_in*)address)->sin_port);
  } else if (address->sa_family == AF_INET6) {
    port = ntohs(((struct sockaddr_in6*)address)->sin6_port);
  } else {
    @throw [NSException exceptionWithName:@"Socket Error"
                                  reason:@"Unknown network type"
                                userInfo:nil];
  }
  return port;
}
```

This bit of C code determines whether the address received from the NSSocketPort is IPv4 or IPv6 and based on that decision extracts the port information from the address and returns it to the caller.

With the port number in hand, we next construct an NSConnection and assign the AppDelegate as the root object. The root object is what will be "proxied" to any clients, and any methods they call on that proxy object will be transferred to the root object on the receiver. In a more complex example, it would make sense to have a separate object used as the proxy instead of the AppDelegate. With the NSConnection created, we can initialize the NSNetService. The NSNetService is what handles the broadcasting using Bonjour. Bonjour requires four pieces of information: the domain, type, name, and port. The port we discovered previously, and the domain and type we defined within the PPDistributed-Protcol. The last value is the name of server and should be unique per machine. With this information, we can instantiate the NSNetService, set its delegate, and publish it. Once we call -publish, other machines can see the service.

Starting the Server

The -startBroadcasting method is invoked from -applicationDidFinishLanching:

DistributedCDServer/AppDelegate.m

```
- (void)applicationDidFinishLaunching:(NSNotification*)notification
{
  [self startBroadcasting];

  saveTimer = [NSTimer scheduledTimerWithTimeInterval:5.0
                                      target:self
                                      selector:@selector(saveAction:)
                                      userInfo:nil
                                       repeats:YES];
}
```

In addition to broadcasting the service on startup, we also schedule an autosave of the NSManagedObjectContext. In this example, we automatically save every five minutes:

DistributedCDServer/AppDelegate.m

```
- (IBAction)saveAction:(id)sender
{
  NSError *error = nil;
  NSManagedObjectContext *context = [self managedObjectContext];
  if (![context hasChanges]) return;
  if (![context save:&error]) {
    [self logError:error];
  }
}
```

The -saveAction: is similar to a save we would see in any Core Data application. There are a couple of changes that we made just for protection. Before we attempt a save call, we first check to see whether there are any changes to save. In addition, instead of handing off the error (if there is one) to the NSApplication to present via the UI, we instead log the error to the console via a call to -logError:. By logging the error, we can see all the issues in a more programmer-friendly setup.

DistributedCDServer/AppDelegate.m

```objc
- (void)logError:(NSError*)error
{
  id sub = [[error userInfo] valueForKey:@"NSUnderlyingException"];

  if (!sub) {
    sub = [[error userInfo] valueForKey:NSUnderlyingErrorKey];
  }

  if (!sub) {
    NSLog(@"%@:%s Error Received: %@", [self class], _cmd,
          [error localizedDescription]);
    return;
  }

  if ([sub isKindOfClass:[NSArray class]] ||
      [sub isKindOfClass:[NSSet class]]) {
    for (NSError *subError in sub) {
      NSLog(@"%@:%s SubError: %@", [self class], _cmd,
            [subError localizedDescription]);
    }
  } else {
    NSLog(@"%@:%s exception %@", [self class], _cmd, [sub description]);
  }
}
```

The -logError: attempts to extract the NSUnderlyingException from the user-Info of the passed-in NSError. If something goes wrong within Core Data that is not part of the normal failure path, it is possible to get information about the failure via the NSUnderlyingException stored. If there is no NSUnderlyingException, then we look for a value stored under the key NSUnderlyingErrorKey. If we get something back from that key, we check to see whether it is a collection, which would indicate multiple validation errors and print the -localizedDescription to the console. If we cannot locate either an NSUnderlyingException or an NSUnderlyingErrorKey, then we dump the -localizedDescription for the NSError that is passed in.

Once the Bonjour service has started and the save thread has started, the server waits for requests from clients. In a distributed object application, the server does not get notified when a client connects; it simply starts getting calls to the exposed methods.

Receiving Requests from Clients

Working with distributed objects is deceptively easy. Other than the minor changes to the method signatures, there are no other changes to the methods and how they are handled. However, whenever we write a method that is going to be accessed via distributed objects, we need to remember that it is not being called locally and keep a few things in mind:

- The server configuration we have built in this example has one incoming socket. That means that it can process only one request at a time. If a request takes too long (which we demonstrate in a moment), all the other clients wait in line; this includes calls from the same client.

- Although we can pass objects by reference to the client, if those objects get passed back to the server by reference, it can cause confusion. This is especially true when dealing with NSManagedObject objects. Therefore, whenever we receive an NSManagedObject back from the client, we resolve a local reference and perform any actions on the local reference instead of trying to use the client reference a second time on the server.

-ping Implementation

The first method I always implement when building a distributed object application is -ping. I use this method to test the connectivity between the client and the server. Since this method does nothing other than print out a console message, I am guaranteed that no other programming errors will be introduced while I test the connectivity.

DistributedCDServer/AppDelegate.m

```
- (oneway void)ping
{
  NSLog(@"%@:%s received", [self class], _cmd);
}
```

-allObjects Implementation

This is one of those methods that is at risk of taking too long:

DistributedCDServer/AppDelegate.m

```
- (byref NSArray*)allObjects
{
  NSManagedObjectContext *context = [self managedObjectContext];
  NSFetchRequest *request = [[NSFetchRequest alloc] init];
  NSEntityDescription *entity = [NSEntityDescription entityForName:@"Test"
                                          inManagedObjectContext:context];
  [request setEntity:entity];

  NSError *error = nil;
```

> ## Joe Asks...
>
> ### Can We Pass the NSManagedObjectContext by Reference?
>
> Although this is feasible, it is not recommended. When we pass objects by reference, a proxy object is created on the receiver that sends all messages back to the server to be performed. This is fine for objects with low complexity, but when dealing with highly complex objects, such as the NSManagedObjectContext, it will perform rather poorly. During experimentation, I received some very unusual errors deep within the Core Data API when the NSManagedObjectContext was passed by reference. Therefore, I do not recommend this approach.

```
  NSArray *objects = [context executeFetchRequest:request error:&error];
  [request release], request = nil;

  if (error) {
    NSLog(@"%@:%s error: %@", [self class], _cmd, error);
    return nil;
  }
  return objects;
}
```

In this method, we retrieve a reference to the NSManagedObjectContext and build an NSFetchRequest to retrieve all the Test entities from the persistent store. If there are any errors, we log them and return nil. Otherwise, we return the resulting NSArray.

This method, although useful for demonstrating distributed objects and Core Data, is a very poor performer. When we start working with tens of thousands of entities in the persistent store, they take a long time to pass over the network. This will hamper the performance of not just the client making the request but of every client waiting in line to make a request on the server. If our requirements involve data of this size, then we should consider other options. One that has met great success is to keep a local copy of the entire repository on each machine and when they sync to merely pass deltas back and forth instead of a true client-server environment.

-createObject Implementation

`DistributedCDServer/AppDelegate.m`

```objc
- (byref NSManagedObject*)createObject;
{
  NSManagedObjectContext *context = [self managedObjectContext];
  NSManagedObject *object = nil;
  object = [NSEntityDescription insertNewObjectForEntityForName:@"Test"
                                     inManagedObjectContext:context];
  return object;
}
```

The -createObject method demonstrates a more performant distributed object method. In this method, we again retrieve a reference the NSManagedObjectContext and then use that reference to create a new Test object. We create and delete all objects on the server as opposed to pulling the NSManagedObjectContext over to the client and trying to delete it remotely. This helps prevent any threading issues while working with the NSManagedObjectContext.

-deleteObject Implementation

`DistributedCDServer/AppDelegate.m`

```objc
- (oneway void)deleteObject:(byref NSManagedObject*)object;
{
  NSManagedObjectContext *context = [self managedObjectContext];
  NSManagedObject *local = [context objectWithID:[object objectID]];
  if ([local isDeleted]) {
    return;
  }
  if (![local isInserted]) {
    [self saveAction:self];
  }
  [context deleteObject:local];
}
```

The -deleteObject is similar to the -createObject discussed earlier. However, in this method, we need to retrieve a local reference to a passed-in NSManagedObject. If we attempted to delete the referenced NSManagedObject directly, the NSManagedObjectContext implodes deep within the API. No doubt this is caused by the double proxy of looping to the remote and then back again to the server. To solve this issue, we retrieve the NSManagedObjetID from the referenced NSManagedObject and use it to retrieve a local reference to the NSManagedObject via the -objectWithID: of the NSManagedObjectContext. Once we have a local reference to the NSManagedObjet, we check to see whether it is freshly inserted or already deleted. If it is freshly inserted, we need to persist it before we can delete it. Therefore, we save the NSManagedObjectContext and then delete the NSManagedObject. If the NSManagedObject has already been deleted, then we return to the caller.

-createChildForObject: Implementation

DistributedCDServer/AppDelegate.m

```
- (byref NSManagedObject*)createChildForObject:(byref NSManagedObject*)parent;
{
  NSManagedObjectContext *context = [self managedObjectContext];
  NSManagedObject *localParent = [context objectWithID:[parent objectID]];
  NSManagedObject *object = nil;
  object = [NSEntityDescription insertNewObjectForEntityForName:@"Child"
                                      inManagedObjectContext:context];
  [object setValue:localParent forKey:@"parent"];
  return object;
}
```

The -createChildForObject: implementation is similar to the -createObject implementation discussed earlier. There is one important difference, though. Since we defined the Child entity to have a nonoptional parent property, we set it immediately while we are still on the main thread of the server. This again is a protection against the uncontrollably multithreaded nature of distributed objects. We could just create the Child entity and return it to the caller, but there is a fair chance that a save will occur before the relationship is updated on the client and an error would result.

In addition to setting the parent property on the Child object, we also grab a local reference to the passed-in NSManagedObject. Although I did not receive any errors during testing of this method by using the remote proxy, there is no reason to risk it.

-objectsOfName:withPredicate: Implementation

DistributedCDServer/AppDelegate.m

```
- (byref NSArray*)objectsOfName:(bycopy NSString*)name
                withPredicate:(bycopy NSPredicate*)predicate;
{
  NSManagedObjectContext *context = [self managedObjectContext];
  NSError *error = nil;
  NSFetchRequest *request = [[NSFetchRequest alloc] init];
  [request setEntity:[NSEntityDescription entityForName:name
                                 inManagedObjectContext:context]];
  [request setPredicate:predicate];
  NSArray *results = [context executeFetchRequest:request error:&error];
  [request release], request = nil;
```

```
  if (error) {
    NSLog(@"%@:%s Error on fetch %@", [self class], _cmd, error);
    return nil;
  }
  return results;
}
```

In this last example method, we deal with a more complicated situation. During the development of this method, I started with passing an NSFetchRequest around between the server and clients. This resulted in some terminal errors within the Core Data stack and led me to this solution instead. Based on these experiments, it is clear to me that passing around the NSManagedObjectContext itself results in some risky situations and should be avoided. However, NSPredicate objects can be passed around without any issue. Therefore, in this method, we accept the name of the entity and the NSPredicate to use in the NSFetchRequest. From this we build the NSFetchRequest and execute it against the local NSManagedObjetContext. If there is an error, we print it to the console and return nil. Otherwise, we return the resulting array.

11.2 Building the Client

The client side of this application is both easier and more complicated than the server. Configuring Bonjour and setting up the distributed objects is a bit more complicated than it is on the server. However, once the distributed object is configured, the rest is significantly easier.

In this example, we are going to build a client that is designed to stress test the server as opposed to being truly functional in a user perspective. Our client is going to connect to the first server that it finds, and once the connection is complete, it will run NSTimer objects to fire against each of the methods on the server in quick succession. With this type of client, we can stress test the server with multiple clients and look for race conditions and threading/locking issues.

Configuring the Xcode Project

Unlike the server, the client is going to start with a Cocoa non–Core Data application. Because the server is maintaining the Core Data repository, the client does not need to be configured as a Core Data application. However, like the server, our user interface is a single window with a single table displaying the results of one of the method calls to the server. See Figure 11.3, on the next page.

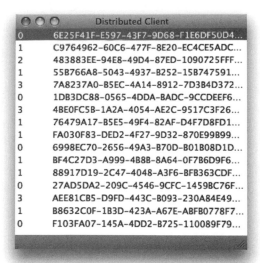

Figure 11.3: THE DISTRIBUTED CLIENT USER INTERFACE

Once the DistributedCDClient project has been created, we need copy the PPDistributedProtocol.h file from the server into the project. Normally I would just reference the file directly from the server project so that both are using the same file, but the example has a copy in each project to prevent any errors in the referencing. Next we need create a new class called AppDelegate and add it to the project. Once the AppDelegate has been added to the project, we will need to configure the user interface.

Opening the MainMenu.xib file in Interface Builder, we will want to add a new NSObject to the xib and set its class to AppDelegate. We then need to bind the NSApplication delegate outlet to the AppDelegate. Next we need to add an NSArrayController to the xib and bind its content array to the AppDelegate with a model key of filteredObjects. Lastly, we need to add an NSTableView to the window, expanding it to take up the entire window and assigning the first column to the NSArrayController with a controller key of arrangedObjects and the model key path set to child-Count. The second column's value should also be set to the NSArrayController with a controller key of arrangedObjects and the model key path set to name. Once that is complete, we can close Interface Builder and open the AppDelegate.

-applicationDidFinishLaunching: Implementation

Like most application delegate objects, our custom code will start in the -applicationDidFinishLaunching:. The first thing that our client needs to do is find a server to connect to. To accomplish this, we initialize an NSNetServiceBrowser and set our AppDelegate as its delegate. We then configure it to search for our server using the #define settings in the protocol that we imported. That browser will then run in the background and start searching for servers on the local network. If it finds a server, it will call -netServiceBrowser:didFindService:moreComing:.

`DistributedCDClient/AppDelegate.m`

```
- (void)applicationDidFinishLaunching:(NSNotification*)notification
{
  NSNetServiceBrowser *myBrowser = [[NSNetServiceBrowser alloc] init];
  [myBrowser setDelegate:self];
  [myBrowser searchForServicesOfType:kServiceName inDomain:kDomainName];
}
```

-netServiceBrowser:didFindService: Implementation

Every time that the NSNetServiceBrowser finds a service, it will call this method. If it finds more than one server in a single sweep of the network, then it will call this method once per service, and the didFindService: will be set to YES.

`DistributedCDClient/AppDelegate.m`

```
- (void)netServiceBrowser:(NSNetServiceBrowser*)browser
           didFindService:(NSNetService*)service
              moreComing:(BOOL)more
{
  [service retain];
  [service setDelegate:self];
  [service resolveWithTimeout:5.0];
  [service startMonitoring];

  [browser stop];
  [browser release], browser = nil;
}
```

In our implementation, as soon as we find a server, we want to connect to it. We are not worried about multiple servers on the network, so the first one that comes in will do. Once we receive notice that a service matching our search criteria is available, we start monitoring it. This will cause the NSNetServiceBrowser to attempt to resolve the service. Once the service is resolved, the service's delegate will receive notification. Therefore, we set the AppDelegate as the delegate to the service. Since we care about only a single service, we shut down the browser and release it.

-netServiceDidResolveAddress: Implementation

Once the service has been resolved, the NSNetService will call -netService-DidResolveAddress: on its delegate. When this method is called, we can retrieve the address and port information about the service, which will let us connect to it and begin using distributed objects.

```
DistributedCDClient/AppDelegate.m
- (void)netServiceDidResolveAddress:(NSNetService*)service
{
  NSConnection *clientConnection = nil;
  NSSocketPort *socket = nil;
  NSData *address = [[service addresses] lastObject];
  u_char family = ((struct sockaddr*)[address bytes])->sa_family;
  socket = [[NSSocketPort alloc] initRemoteWithProtocolFamily:family
                                        socketType:SOCK_STREAM
                                          protocol:IPPROTO_TCP
                                           address:address];
  clientConnection = [NSConnection connectionWithReceivePort:nil
                                             sendPort:socket];
  [clientConnection enableMultipleThreads];
  server = [clientConnection rootProxy];

  [socket release], socket = nil;
  [service stop];
  [service release];

  [self startTestTimers];
}
```

Once the NSNetService has been resolved, we can retrieve its addresses and connect to it. With access to the address from the NSNetService, we can initialize an NSSocketPort to connect to the server hosting the service. With the NSSocketPort initialized, we can then initialize an NSConnection and finally get a reference to the -rootProxy of the NSConnection, which is actually an NSDistantObject proxy for the AppDelegate of the server. Once we have the server referenced properly, we can shut down the Bonjour NSNetService and start our tests.

11.3 Testing the Networking Code

Whenever I build an application that needs to communicate to a server or another device, I always start off with simple tests to confirm that the connection is working. I generally leave these tests in place until the code goes to production. This both provides me with a simple way to test the connectivity and gives me a base to fall back upon if some of the higher-level functions start to fail. For this application, we will start with setting up a group of timers that will fire off our test methods.

-startTestTimers Implementation

To simulate a large amount of client-server traffic, this application runs several timers at a fairly high pace. This will help us catch any race conditions or other issues with the distributed nature of this application.

`DistributedCDClient/AppDelegate.m`

```objc
- (void)startTestTimers
{
  SEL selector = @selector(testPing);
  pingTimer = [NSTimer scheduledTimerWithTimeInterval:0.5
                                               target:self
                                             selector:selector
                                             userInfo:nil
                                              repeats:YES];

  selector = @selector(testObjectInsertion);
  insertTimer = [NSTimer scheduledTimerWithTimeInterval:0.5
                                                 target:self
                                               selector:selector
                                               userInfo:nil
                                                repeats:YES];

  selector = @selector(testObjectDeletion);
  deleteTimer = [NSTimer scheduledTimerWithTimeInterval:1.0
                                                 target:self
                                               selector:selector
                                               userInfo:nil
                                                repeats:YES];

  selector = @selector(testChildInsertion);
  childInsertTimer = [NSTimer scheduledTimerWithTimeInterval:1.0
                                                      target:self
                                                    selector:selector
                                                    userInfo:nil
                                                     repeats:YES];

  selector = @selector(testChildDeletion);
  childDeleteTimer = [NSTimer scheduledTimerWithTimeInterval:1.0
                                                      target:self
                                                    selector:selector
                                                    userInfo:nil
                                                     repeats:YES];
```

```
    selector = @selector(testObjectFetch);
    fetchTimer = [NSTimer scheduledTimerWithTimeInterval:15.0
                                                  target:self
                                                selector:selector
                                                userInfo:nil
                                                 repeats:YES];
}
```

The -startTestTimers fires up a number of timers that will continuously call our test methods. We retain a reference to each of these timers so that we can later shut them down gracefully.

-disconnect Implementation

Whenever we shut down the client application, we want to shut down the timers, and we want to close the connection to the server. The -disconnect walks through each of the NSTimer references and invalidates them. Once all the timers are shut down, it then retrieves the NSConnection from the server proxy and invalidates it.

DistributedCDClient/AppDelegate.m

```
- (void)disconnect
{
    [pingTimer invalidate], pingTimer = nil;
    [fetchTimer invalidate], fetchTimer = nil;
    [insertTimer invalidate], insertTimer = nil;
    [deleteTimer invalidate], deleteTimer = nil;
    [childDeleteTimer invalidate], childDeleteTimer = nil;
    [childInsertTimer invalidate], childInsertTimer = nil;

    NSConnection *connection = [(NSDistantObject*)server connectionForProxy];
    [connection invalidate];
    server = nil;
}
```

-testPing Implementation

The first of our test methods is also the simplest. We call the -ping method on the server and nothing else. We do not expect a return from the server at all. What this method will do is cause a log statement to be generated on the server. This allows us to watch the server and see that connections are in fact coming in. The other benefit is that it keeps the testing simple. With this method, we can confirm that the Bonjour service and the distributed objects are working properly without having to wonder whether some other logic in some other part of our application is the real source of a failure. If the ping is not getting through, we know that either the Bonjour service or the distributed objects are failing.

```
- (void)testPing
{
  [server ping];
}
```

-testObjectFetch Implementation

The -testObjectFetch is the first complicated method that we are testing across the distributed objects link. In this test, we construct an NSPredicate that we pass to the server to be executed against the NSManagedObjectContext. As I mentioned, passing the NSManagedObjectContext itself across distributed objects produced some terminal exceptions within the Core Data stack itself, so we are avoiding this by performing as much of the Core Data work as possible on the server. Here we are passing in the name of the entity we want to search against and the NSPredicate. The server will return an NSArray of the entities that fit the NSPredicate. One interesting thing to note in this method is that we are not using the new for loop to access the returned NSArray. Since the NSArray is actually an NSDistant proxy for the NSArray on the server, the new for loop does not handle it properly. Therefore, we need to use the older NSEnumerator instead.

```
- (void)testObjectFetch
{
  NSString *test = [GUID substringToIndex:3];
  NSPredicate *predicate = nil;
  predicate = [NSPredicate predicateWithFormat:@"name contains[c] %@", test];

  NSArray *results = [server objectsOfName:@"Test" withPredicate:predicate];

  NSEnumerator *enumerator = [results objectEnumerator];
  NSManagedObject *object;
  while (object = [enumerator nextObject]) {
    [object setValue:GUID forKey:@"name"];
  }

  [self setFilteredObjects:results];
}
```

To show and test KVO across the distributed objects, we loop over the NSManagedObject objects within the NSArray and update their name to a globally unique string that we retrieve from NSProcessInfo using a #define to make it a little easier to read. The #define is as follows:

```
#define GUID [[NSProcessInfo processInfo] globallyUniqueString]
```

-testObjectInsertion Implementation

Testing object creation is only a single call to the server. However, to test that we can start using the object immediately, we also set its name using a globally unique string received from the NSProcessInfo. In addition, we also added a random into this method so that approximately 50 percent of the time it would not do an insertion. This adds a bit of randomness into the data testing and helps keep the number of Test entities on the server low.

DistributedCDClient/AppDelegate.m

```
- (void)testObjectInsertion
{
  if ((rand() % 2) == NO) return;
  NSManagedObject *object = [server createObject];
  [object setValue:GUID forKey:@"name"];
}
```

-testObjectDeletion Implementation

-testObjectDeletion is a fair bit more complicated than -testObjectInsertion because we need to have a reference to an object first before we can delete it. Therefore, this method starts off by calling -allObjects on the server to get an NSArray of Test entities. From that NSArray, we randomly select an entity to delete and call -deleteObject: on the server.

DistributedCDClient/AppDelegate.m

```
- (void)testObjectDeletion
{
  NSArray *objects = [server allObjects];

  if (![objects count]) return;

  int index = (rand() % [objects count]);
  NSManagedObject *toBeDeleted = [objects objectAtIndex:index];

  [server deleteObject:toBeDeleted];
}
```

-testChildInsertion Implementation

To test relationships, we have two methods: child creation and child deletion. In the first one, -testChildInsertion, we start off by getting an

NSArray of all the Test entities. From there, we call createChildForObject: on the server, randomly using one of the Test entities from the retrieved NSArray. We let the server handle the actual creation of the relationship between these objects to ensure that there are no issues with the distributed objects themselves. During testing, Core Data got confused when the relationship was created on the client as opposed to the server. Therefore, to avoid any risks in this area, we pass the parent back to the server to let the server both create the child and set the relationship between the two objects.

DistributedCDClient/AppDelegate.m

```
- (void)testChildInsertion
{
  NSArray *objects = [server allObjects];
  id object = [objects objectAtIndex:(rand() % [objects count])];
  id child = [server createChildForObject:object];
  [child setValue:GUID forKey:@"name"];
}
```

-testChildDeletion Implementation

The last test method is the deletion of a child object. In this test, we again retrieve all the Test entities from the server and randomly select one. We then check to see whether the Test entity has a child, and if it does, then we grab one of them and call -deleteObject: on the server with that child as the parameter.

DistributedCDClient/AppDelegate.m

```
- (void)testChildDeletion
{
  NSArray *objects = [server allObjects];

  int index = (rand() % [objects count]);
  id object = [objects objectAtIndex:index];

  NSSet *children = [object valueForKey:@"children"];

  if (![children count]) return;

  id child = [children anyObject];
  [server deleteObject:child];
}
```

11.4 Wrapping Up

Whenever we start working with multiple computers on a network or interapplication communication, the code starts to get extremely complex. However, at least with this design, we can keep the Core Data/ persistence separated from the distributed objects/networking as much as possible. By doing so, we avoid the need for a large number of locks and synchronization that would otherwise be required.

As we discussed at the beginning of this chapter, it is not a very scalable design, but in situations where a formal stand-alone database is overkill, this design actually works quite well. There is no user configuration, and there is no need to set up an external application; we just start one application on one machine and another application on another and let them talk. The biggest gotcha is with the NSManagedObjectContext. As long as we do not try to share it across the distributed objects, we can use Core Data fairly transparently.

The design that we built here can also be used in a peer environment as opposed to the client-server design. Multiple peers could use Bonjour to discover each other and use distributed objects to sync their data stores so that each device has a complete and up-to-date copy of the data set. In a situation like that, a user could have our application on each of their machines, and whenever they are near each other (that is, on the same local network), they would automatically update each other. Talk about a pleasant user experience!

Chapter 12

Recipe: Dynamic Parameters

If you have a document-style application, you will need to work with document-specific parameters or settings. For example, in a word processor, some settings are specific to one document, and some settings apply to the entire application. When it comes to storing application-level parameters, we have a great implementation: NSUserDefaults. However, when it comes to document-level parameters, there is no reusable storage system for them provided by the APIs. In this chapter, we'll build that reusable storage system within Core Data.

System-level and user-level preferences are extremely useful and easy to access on OS X. One call to standardDefaults on NSUserDefaults from anywhere in the application instantly gives you access to the defaults for the currently logged in user. However, sometimes we don't want to store preferences at the user level but would prefer to store them at the file level.

When we are working with a Core Data application, the first thought is to just create a table for these parameters and access them from within the Core Data API. However, the problem comes when we are accessing those parameters. No longer is it a single call to standardDefaults on NSUserDefaults; now it looks more like this:

CDPreferences/MyDocument.m

```
- (void)clunkyParameterAccess
{
  NSManagedObjectContext *moc = [self managedObjectContext];
  NSFetchRequest *request = [[NSFetchRequest alloc] init];
  [request setEntity:[NSEntityDescription entityForName:@"parameter"
                                  inManagedObjectContext:moc]];
```

```
  [request setPredicate:[NSPredicate predicateWithFormat:@"name == %@",
                          @"default1"]];

  NSError *error = nil;

  NSManagedObject *param = [[moc executeFetchRequest:request
                                            error:&error] lastObject];
  if (error) {
    NSLog(@"%@:%s Error fetching param: %@", [self class], _cmd, error);
    return;
  }

  NSLog(@"%@:%s Parameter value %@", [self class], _cmd,
        [param valueForKey:@"value"]);
}
```

Worse is when we need to *set* a parameter:

```
CDPreferences/MyDocument.m
```

```
- (void)clunkyParameterWrite
{
  NSManagedObjectContext *moc = [self managedObjectContext];
  NSFetchRequest *request = [[NSFetchRequest alloc] init];
  [request setEntity:[NSEntityDescription entityForName:@"parameter"
                              inManagedObjectContext:moc]];

  [request setPredicate:[NSPredicate predicateWithFormat:@"name == %@",
                          @"default1"]];

  NSError *error = nil;

  NSManagedObject *param = [[moc executeFetchRequest:request
                                            error:&error] lastObject];
  if (error) {
    NSLog(@"%@:%s Error fetching param: %@", [self class], _cmd, error);
    return;
  }

  if (!param) {
    param = [NSEntityDescription insertNewObjectForEntityForName:@"Parameter"
                                        inManagedObjectContext:moc];
    [param setValue:@"default1" forKey:@"name"];
  }

  [param setValue:@"SomeValue" forKey:@"value"];
}
```

The most obvious solution to this is to abstract away this code somewhere so that we can hit it with only one line of code. Wouldn't it be

nice if we could access our document-level parameters with code like this:

`CDPreferences/MyDocument.m`

```
if ([[[self defaults] valueForKey:@"default1"] boolValue]) {
  //Do something clever
}
```

and be able to set them with something like this:

`CDPreferences/MyDocument.m`

```
[[self defaults] setValue:@"New Value" forKey:@"newKey"];
```

In this example, that is exactly what we are going to do. As we discussed briefly in Chapter 3, *Core Data and Bindings*, on page 27, every object responds to the -valueForUndefinedKey: and -setValue:forUndefinedKey: methods. We can use (or abuse) these methods and make them do all of the heavy lifting for us.

12.1 Building the Xcode Example Project

To start this project, we'll use the Core Data Document-based Application template from within Xcode. In a document-based application, each document object has its own Core Data stack as opposed to having a single Core Data stack for the entire application.

Once we have created the project, named CDPreferences, we need to create the data model. For this example, we are going to focus only on the parameters and build the parameters table shown in Figure 12.1, on the next page. Each parameter has two properties; a name that is a nonoptional string and a value that is an optional string. By making the value optional, we can have parameters that are nullable.

With no additional code changes, our application will correctly start up and display an empty document. Since each document has its own persistent store, the persistent store becomes the document that is being saved to disk. The next step is to build the object that will manage the parameters.

12.2 The DocumentPreferences Object

To build a system that imitates the NSUserDefaults, we need to have a single object that manages the parameters table for us. By doing so, we can treat the entire parameters table as if it were a single object with

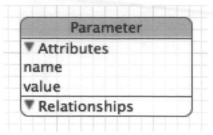

Figure 12.1: Parameter table model

a dynamic number of accessors. However, we do not want to have to write an accessor every time that we add a parameter; ideally, we want to just call -valueForKey: and -setValue:forKey: and not worry about the persistence of these values. Lastly, we want to be able to set up some default values.

An important point about the defaults is that they are not persisted to disk. If they get persisted, then later versions that change the default would require additional code to check for persisted defaults and reset them. If, however, we do not persist them, then users of newer versions of the application automatically get the newer defaults for free and, more important, do not get their preferences destroyed if they have changed the value from its default.

The DocumentPreferences object will accomplish all of these goals:

```
CDPreferences/DocumentPreferences.h
@interface DocumentPreferences : NSObject
{
  NSDictionary *_defaults;
  NSPersistentDocument *_associatedDocument;
}

@property (assign) NSPersistentDocument *associatedDocument;
@property (assign) NSDictionary *defaults;

- (id)initWithDocument:(NSPersistentDocument*)associatedDocument;
- (NSArray*)allParameterNames;
- (NSDictionary*)allParameters;

@end
```

Our DocumentPreferences object expects to receive a reference to its NSPersistentDocument upon initialization. From the passed-in reference, our DocumentPreferences will be able to access the underlying NSManagedObjectContext. We could also just incorporate this design directly into a subclass of NSPersistentDocument; however, that can cause the document object to become quite large and difficult to maintain. Therefore, even though there is a one-to-one relationship between NSPersistentDocument objects and DocumentPreferences objects, we keep them separate to reduce code complexity.

The one thing that's missing from this header file is any way to access the parameters themselves. There are no methods for this access because we are going to take advantage of KVC. Whenever another piece of code requests a parameter from our DocumentPreferences object, the -valueForUndefinedKey: method will get called, and that is where we handle access to the parameters table.

-valueForUndefinedKey:

CDPreferences/DocumentPreferences.m

```
- (id)valueForUndefinedKey:(NSString*)key
{
  id parameter = [self findParameter:key];
  if (!parameter && [[self defaults] objectForKey:key]) {
    return [[self defaults] objectForKey:key];
  }
  return [parameter valueForKey:@"value"];
}
```

In this method, we receive the name of the value that the caller is attempting to retrieve. We use this name to retrieve the NSManagedObject via the -findParameter: method and return the NSManagedObject object's value property. If there is no parameter with the passed-in name, then we check the defaults NSDictionary to see whether there is a default for it. If there is no default set, we let the -valueForKey: method return nil to the caller.

-findParameter:

CDPreferences/DocumentPreferences.m

```
- (NSManagedObject*)findParameter:(NSString*)name;
{
  NSManagedObjectContext *moc;
  NSManagedObject *param;
  NSError *error = nil;
  moc = [[self associatedDocument] managedObjectContext];
```

```
NSFetchRequest *request = [[NSFetchRequest alloc] init];
[request setEntity:[NSEntityDescription entityForName:@"Parameter"
                              inManagedObjectContext:moc]];
[request setPredicate:[NSPredicate predicateWithFormat:@"name == %@", name]];

param = [[moc executeFetchRequest:request error:&error] lastObject];
if (error) {
  NSLog(@"%@:%s Error fetching parameter: %@", [self class], _cmd, error);
  return nil;
}
[request release], request = nil;
return param;
}
```

In the -findParameter: method, we construct an NSFetchRequest against the parameters table using a compare on the name property to filter it down to a single result. Assuming there is no error on the fetch, we return the NSManagedObject that is returned. In this method, we are using the -lastObject method on the resulting array as a convenience. -lastObject automatically checks for an empty array and will return nil if the array is empty. This reduces the code complexity and gives us the result we want in a single call. If there is an error accessing the Core Data stack, we report the error and return nil. Note that we do not create a parameter if there is not one in this method. We intentionally separate this out so that we are not creating potentially empty parameters. This allows us to request a parameter and check whether it is nil without concern of parameters being generated unnecessarily.

-setValue:forUndefinedKey:

CDPreferences/DocumentPreferences.m

```
- (void)setValue:(id)value forUndefinedKey:(NSString*)key
{
  [self willChangeValueForKey:key];
  NSManagedObject *parameter = [self findParameter:key];
  if (!parameter) {
    if ([[self defaults] valueForKey:key] &&
        [value isEqualTo:[[self defaults] valueForKey:key]]) {
      [self didChangeValueForKey:key];
      return;
    }
    parameter = [self createParameter:key];
  } else {
    if ([[self defaults] valueForKey:key] &&
        [value isEqualTo:[[self defaults] valueForKey:key]]) {
      [self didChangeValueForKey:key];
      [[[self associatedDocument] managedObjectContext] deleteObject:parameter];
```

```
      [self didChangeValueForKey:key];
      return;
    }
  }

  if ([value isKindOfClass:[NSNumber class]]) {
    [parameter setValue:[value stringValue] forKey:@"value"];
  } else if ([value isKindOfClass:[NSDate class]]) {
    [parameter setValue:[value description] forKey:@"value"];
  } else {
    [parameter setValue:value forKey:@"value"];
  }
  [self didChangeValueForKey:key];
}
```

In addition to being able to access a parameter, we also need to set parameters. This is done in the counterpart method of -valueForUn-definedKey: called -setValue:forUndefinedKey:. In this method, we first notify the system that we are going to be changing the value associated with the passed-in key. This is part of KVO and is required so that notifications work correctly. After starting the KVO notification, we attempt to retrieve the NSManagedObject from the parameters table. If there is no NSManagedObject for the passed-in key, we then check the defaults NSDictionary to see whether there is a default. If there is a default set and the passed-in value matches the default, we complete the KVO notification and return. If the default value does not match the passed-in value, we create a new NSManagedObject for the passed-in key.

If there is an NSManagedObject and a default set for the key, we compare the default value to the passed-in value. If they match, we then *delete* the NSManagedObject, which effectively resets the parameter to the default. Once we pass the checks against default and/or create the NSManagedObject, we test the value to see whether it is an NSNumber or NSDate. If it is, then we pass in its -stringValue or -description as the value for the NSManagedObject. Otherwise, we pass in the value directly to the NSManagedObject. Once the value is set, we call -didChangeValueForKey: to complete the KVO notification.

-createParameter:

CDPreferences/DocumentPreferences.m

```
- (NSManagedObject*)createParameter:(NSString*)name
{
  NSManagedObject *param;
  NSManagedObjectContext *moc;
```

```
    moc = [[self associatedDocument] managedObjectContext];
    param = [NSEntityDescription insertNewObjectForEntityForName:@"Parameter"
                                    inManagedObjectContext:moc];
    [param setValue:name forKey:@"name"];
    return param;
}
```

The -createParameter: method creates a new NSManagedObject and sets
the name property with the passed-in value. It does not set the value
property, leaving that up to the caller. This allows us to set a nil parameter if we really need one.

-allParameters

`CDPreferences/DocumentPreferences.m`

```
- (NSDictionary*)allParameters;
{
    NSManagedObjectContext *moc;
    NSError *error = nil;
    moc = [[self associatedDocument] managedObjectContext];
    NSFetchRequest *request = [[NSFetchRequest alloc] init];
    [request setEntity:[NSEntityDescription entityForName:@"Parameter"
                                    inManagedObjectContext:moc]];
    NSArray *params = [moc executeFetchRequest:request error:&error];
    if (error) {
        NSLog(@"%@:%s Error fetching parameter: %@", [self class], _cmd, error);
        return nil;
    }

    NSMutableDictionary *dict = [[self defaults] mutableCopy];
    for (NSManagedObject *param in params) {
        NSString *name = [param valueForKey:@"name"];
        NSString *value = [param valueForKey:@"value"];
        [dict setValue: value forKey:name];
    }
    return dict;
}
```

In addition to the primary function of this class, we have a couple of
convenience methods that have proven useful. The first one, -allPara-
meters, returns an NSDictionary of all the parameters, including the defaults. In this method, we create an NSFetchRequest for the Parameter
entity without an NSPredicate. We take the resulting NSArray from the
fetch and loop over it. Within that loop, we add each NSManagedObject to an NSMutableDictionary derived from the default NSDictionary. This
ensures that we have both the default values and the Parameter entries
included in the final NSDictionary.

-allParameterNames

`CDPreferences/DocumentPreferences.m`

```objc
- (NSArray*)allParameterNames;
{
  NSManagedObjectContext *moc;
  NSError *error = nil;
  moc = [[self associatedDocument] managedObjectContext];
  NSFetchRequest *request = [[NSFetchRequest alloc] init];
  [request setEntity:[NSEntityDescription entityForName:@"Parameter"
                                 inManagedObjectContext:moc]];
  NSArray *params = [moc executeFetchRequest:request error:&error];
  if (error) {
    NSLog(@"%@:%s Error fetching parameter: %@", [self class], _cmd, error);
    return nil;
  }

  NSMutableArray *keys = [[[self defaults] allKeys] mutableCopy];
  for (NSManagedObject *param in params) {
    NSString *name = [param valueForKey:@"name"];
    [keys addObject:name];
  }
  return keys;
}
```

Like -allParameters, -allParameterNames is a convenience method that returns an NSArray of the keys currently set or defaulted. Just like the
-allParameters method, it retrieves all the parameter NSManagedObject
objects and loops over them. Within that loop, it adds the name property
to an NSMutableArray derived from the defaultsNSDictionary.

12.3 Review

With this design, we can access our parameters within each document
without having to worry about the underlying structure. We also don't
need to stop coding just to hop over and add a parameter to the object.
We can work with DocumentPreferences in the same manner that we
work with NSUserDefaults.

This same design can be used in a nondocument application by changing the DocumentPreferences object into a singleton or by adding the
-valueForUndefinedKey: and -setValue:forUndefinedKey: methods directly to
the NSApplication delegate along with the NSManagedObjectContext.

Whether we are working in a document model or not, we can now access persistent store–specific parameters with a single call similar to the following:

```
NSString *value = [[self preferences] valueForKey:@"exampleKey1"];
```

We can also set them with a call similar to the following:

```
[[self preferences] setValue:@"someValue" forKey:@"someKey"];
```

In both of these examples, we are calling -valueForKey: and -setValue:for-Key: directly on the DocumentPreferences object and not worrying about whether the value exists. If it does not exist, we will receive a nil. If it has been set as a default, we will get the default back, and if we have overridden the default or previously set the property, it will be returned.

Lastly, like the NSUserDefaults, the default values are not persisted to disk. Therefore, we need to set them every time we initialize the DocumentPreferences:

CDPreferences/MyDocument.m

```
NSMutableDictionary *defaults = [NSMutableDictionary dictionary];
[defaults setValue:[NSNumber numberWithBool:YES] forKey:@"default1"];
[defaults setValue:@"DefaultValue2" forKey:@"default2"];
[defaults setValue:@"DefaultValue3" forKey:@"default3"];
[_preferences setDefaults:defaults];
```

However, we do not need to worry about changing the defaults at a later date. If we change the defaults in a subsequent version, they will automatically be updated if the user has not overridden them.

Index

T

U

More Mac OS X Titles...

For more books and screencasts on XCode, Cocoa, the iPhone, TextMate and other Mac topics, please visit www.pragprog.com.

Cocoa Programming

Cocoa Programming shows you how to get productive with Cocoa–fast! You'll learn to use the Apple developer tools to design your user interface, write the code, and create the data model. We'll show you Objective-C concepts when you are ready to apply them throughout the book. By the end of the book, you'll be a Cocoa programmer.

Cocoa Programming: A Quick-Start Guide for Developers
Daniel H Steinberg
(280 pages) ISBN: 978-19343563-0-2. $32.95
http://pragprog.com/titles/dscpq

Core Animation for OS X/iPhone

Have you seen Apple's Front Row application and Cover Flow effects? Then you've seen Core Animation at work. It's about making applications that give strong visual feedback through movement and morphing, rather than repainting panels. This comprehensive guide will get you up to speed quickly and take you into the depths of this new technology.

Core Animation for Mac OS X and the iPhone: Creating Compelling Dynamic User Interfaces
Bill Dudney
(220 pages) ISBN: 978-1-9343561-0-4. $34.95
http://pragprog.com/titles/bdcora

The Pragmatic Bookshelf

The Pragmatic Bookshelf features books written by developers for developers. The titles continue the well-known Pragmatic Programmer style and continue to garner awards and rave reviews. As development gets more and more difficult, the Pragmatic Programmers will be there with more titles and products to help you stay on top of your game.

Visit Us Online

Core Data's Home Page
http://pragprog.com/titles/mzcd
Source code from this book, errata, and other resources. Come give us feedback, too!

Register for Updates
http://pragprog.com/updates
Be notified when updates and new books become available.

Join the Community
http://pragprog.com/community
Read our weblogs, join our online discussions, participate in our mailing list, interact with our wiki, and benefit from the experience of other Pragmatic Programmers.

New and Noteworthy
http://pragprog.com/news
Check out the latest pragmatic developments, new titles and other offerings.

Save on the eBook

Save on the eBook versions of this title. Owning the paper version of this book entitles you to purchase the electronic versions at a terrific discount.

PDFs are great for carrying around on your laptop—they are hyperlinked, have color, and are fully searchable. Most titles are also available for the iPhone and iPod touch, Amazon Kindle, and other popular e-book readers.

Buy now at pragprog.com/coupon.

Contact Us

Online Orders:	www.pragprog.com/catalog
Customer Service:	support@pragprog.com
Non-English Versions:	translations@pragprog.com
Pragmatic Teaching:	academic@pragprog.com
Author Proposals:	proposals@pragprog.com
Contact us:	1-800-699-PROG (+1 919 847 3884)